# DORSET

*Above* Cottage at Stanbridge

*Following page* Lewesdon Hill from Pilsdon Pen.
At 915 feet (279 metres), the wooded summit
of Lewesdon Hill is Dorset's highest point.

# DORSET

## THE COUNTY IN COLOUR

*Photographs by*

JULIAN COMRIE

*Text by*

DAVID BURNETT

DOVECOTE PRESS

Looking towards Handfast Point with Swanage Pier
in the foreground. The chalk stack rising from the sea is Old Harry.
He was once partnered by Old Harry's Wife,
but she fell in 1896 and only her stump remains.

First published in 1991 by The Dovecote Press Ltd
Stanbridge, Wimborne, Dorset BH21 4JD

ISBN 0 946159 88 2

Photographs © Julian Comrie 1991
Text © David Burnett 1991

Designed by Humphrey Stone

Photoset in Sabon by The Typesetting Bureau Ltd, Wimborne, Dorset
Origination by Chroma Graphics (Overseas) Pte Ltd, Singapore
Printed and bound by Kim Hup Lee Printing Co Pte Ltd, Singapore

British Library Cataloguing-in-Publication Data
A catalogue record of this book is
available from the British Library

# CONTENTS

# DORSET

King George III chose the sea off a Dorset beach to first 'pop his royal head underwater', Charles II thought no countryside finer than the Marshwood Vale, Sir Walter Raleigh and Thomas Hardy asked to be buried in the county (apart from Hardy's heart both were denied their wishes), and early visitors praised its beers and 'the mildness of the air and the beauty of its situation'. Yet when attempts were first made to promote a railway into Dorset it was thought that few passengers would think the journey worth the cost of a ticket and that its sole export would be heather for brooms. Today, nearly 150 years later, Dorset is amongst the most visited of counties, and the surviving heathland is just one of the many landscapes that those who know the county would place near the top of any list of its virtues.

For above all else it is Dorset's diversity that has most enriched it. Chalk, clay, sand, gravel and stone are all present, creating a geological cocktail that has shaped every aspect of its past, from architecture to farming to the growth of the towns and villages. But Dorset is a small county, and the packing of so much into so little means that each different landscape is intimate and small-scale.

Nowhere is this more obvious than in the Isle of Purbeck. As well as providing both the site and building stone for Dorset's most famous landmark, Corfe Castle, it combines a range of miniature landscapes – heath, chalk hills, clay vale, limestone plateau descending to the sea – with what must be one of England's most gloriously unspoilt stretches of coast.

Purbeck's beauty makes the contrast with the built-up sprawl that runs eastward for fifteen miles from the entrance of Poole Harbour to the country boundary at Highcliffe even more pronounced. Yet there are compensations. Bournemouth has its beaches, Poole and Christchurch their harbours. Away from the towns the song of the Dartford Warbler can still be heard on the heath.

Once north of Wimborne the landscape changes dramatically. In the Middle Ages Cranborne Chase was a royal hunting preserve whose deer were fought over by both huntsmen and poacher. Blandford and Shaftesbury mark its western rim, but villages are few, and most of the Chase is open down divided by steep wooded combes.

On its western slopes the Chase gives way to the Blackmore Vale, described by Thomas Hardy as being the one part of Dorset where 'the fields are never brown and the springs never dry.' Little has changed since he wrote. Small fields and hedgerow oaks watered by slow-moving rivers still predominate. Farm and woodland spill westward, and the lovely honey-coloured limestone with which much of Sherborne and the surrounding villages are built gives the area its character.

To the south and west lies the Marshood Vale. Smaller than Blackmore, but its equal in

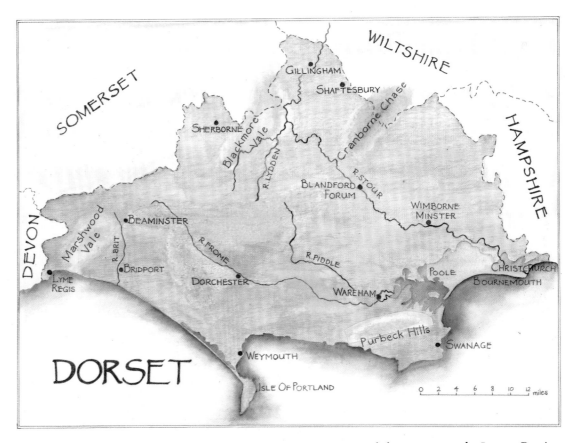

DORSET

beauty, the encircling hills look out over a scattering of farms towards Lyme Regis, Bridport and the distant sea. To the east of Bridport the landscape makes its most abrupt change in the county. A 17th century traveller to Dorset described Chesil Beach as the 'stranger's wonder, the nation's boast'. Sailors thought otherwise, for in the past it was all too often their graveyard. Inland from Weymouth Bay the ground slopes upward, before falling to the heathland bordering the valleys of the Frome and Piddle rivers. But as the Piddle narrows and the Frome swings north beyond Dorchester the landscape changes. For much of the spine of the county, and a third of its total, is rolling chalk downland. Here the villages shelter in the valleys, often alongside the streams that rise on the downs.

Now largely empty, the chalk uplands provide perhaps the best evidence of early man's efforts to settle the county. Neolithic man built circular earthworks such as Maumbury Rings, dug the six mile banks of the enigmatic Dorset Cursus on Cranborne Chase. Round burial barrows mark the birth of the Bronze Age. To the Iron Age we owe Maiden Castle and Hambledon Hill, just two of the thirty spectacular hillforts in the county. The Romans left an amphitheatre and aqueduct, the fine mosaic floors of their villas, as well as one of the best preserved lengths of Roman road in Britain.

By the date of the Norman Conquest the Saxons had founded many of Dorset's towns and villages. In the centuries that followed the sheep grazing the downs brought wealth to the great monastic houses: Sherborne, Forde, Milton, Abbotsbury, Shaftesbury, Cerne, Bindon, and Christchurch. Their Dissolution in the 16th century introduced a new breed of landowner, opportunists whose heirs built many of the small manor houses that remain one of Dorset's glories. Poole and Lyme Regis were besieged in the Civil War, and following its fall by treachery Corfe Castle was slighted. The Duke of Monmouth landed at Lyme before launching his doomed Rebellion in 1685. In its wake many of the rebels were hung, and their quartered limbs put on display throughout the county.

Dorset's subsequent history has been less troubled. George III made Weymouth fashionable, but it was Thomas Hardy, born in 1840 and the son of a small builder and mason, who transformed his native county into a vision of a rural England that still endures to this day. The impact of the twentieth century has inevitably diluted that vision, and yet, as the photographs in this book make apparent, there are few corners that can't be turned without coming across the Dorset described by Hardy. There are no motorways, no large industries outside Bournemouth and Poole. In winter, the towns still retain the somnolent air of the English provincial town.

A book such as this can do no more than give a taste of the county. Yet such is Julian Comrie's quite remarkable skill with a camera that he has seen it through fresh eyes and breathed new life into it. There are people as well as places, and without the former the latter would have no purpose. Of course, not everywhere can be included. Each of us has a handful of favourite spots that sum up Dorset's attractions. On first entering the county more than twenty years ago I became stranded in the ford at Tarrant Monkton, and to this day cannot pass by without thanking the Tarrant's waters for halting me where they did. Few guests are excused the walk out to Swyre Head with Encombe in its bowl on one side and Portland low against the horizon on the other. There is no more breathtaking view than the Blackmore Vale from below Bulbarrow at first light, no finer place for a picnic than Coney's Castle with the Marshwood Vale sloping away to the east. Thanks to the photographs that follow such lists will undoubtedly lengthen, as those of us who think we know the county discover it anew, and those being introduced to it for the first time are able to enjoy its delights.

DAVID BURNETT
*Stanbridge*

# DORCHESTER AND THE CHALK DOWNLAND

# DORCHESTER AND THE
# CHALK DOWNLAND

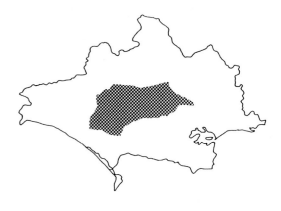

*The zwellen downs, wi' chalky tracks*
*A-climmen up their sunny backs*
*Do hide green meads an zedgy brooks,*
*An' clumps o' trees wi' glossy rooks,*
*An' hearty wo'k to laugh an' zing,*
*An' parish-churches in a string,*
*Wi' tow'rs o' merry bells to ring,*
*An' white roads up athirt the hills.*

So wrote the Dorset poet William Barnes in the 1840s, and, like everything he wrote about his native county, it superbly evokes its atmosphere. Here Barnes is describing a landscape that fills the entire heart of the county, from beyond Dorchester in the west and east to Cranborne Chase, and which, apart from the county town and the two picture-postcard villages of Milton Abbas and Cerne Abbas, is still little-visited.

Dorchester was the Roman Durnovaria, to whose south lay the huge Iron Age hillfort of Maiden Castle, which the Romans stormed after landing. Dorchester's tree-lined Walks were laid out in the 18th Century on the Roman walls, and many of the mosaics unearthed from the pavements and houses of the Roman town can be seen in the County Museum. A vanished castle was built after the Norman conquest, and the town prospered as the cloth trade grew. By the beginning of the 19th century it had survived a series of disastrous fires, whilst the presence of the Assize Court, prison, barracks, and a number of attractive Georgian houses and shops, had given it the bustle that befitted its status. Thomas Hardy described it in *The Mayor of Casterbridge*. 'The farmer's boy could sit under his barley mow and pitch a stone into the office window of the town clerk; reapers at work among the sheaves nodded to acquaintances standing on the street corner; the red-robed judge, when he condemned a sheep stealer, pronounced sentence to the tune of Baa, that floated in at the window from the remainder of the flock grazing hard by.'

Sheep made Dorchester wealthy, and one early visitor thought the surrounding downland white as snow, so vast were the grazing flocks. Although they created the dense downland turf, much is now corn, and, in winter, the high central chalk seems bleak and inhospitable. The villages take shelter in the river valleys, Barnes's 'parish churches in a string'. Typical of these are the two groups of Winterbornes, so named because the streams they straddle dry-up in summer, and the villages that line the Piddle, Cerne and Sydling valleys.

*Previous page* Shoppers pausing for a rest in Cornhill, Dorchester, with the old town pump in the background, and, beyond it, the mid 19th century Corn Exchange.

*Right* The 17th century stone and flint rubble Nether Cerne House and the medieval church of All Saints, formerly a chapel of Cerne Abbas.

*Below* South Walks, Dorchester, with the chestnut trees either side just breaking into leaf. Just visible at the far end are the Dorset Martyrs, three bronze figures by Elisabeth Frink, which stand on the site of the gallows as a memorial to those who suffered religious persecution. The Walks are one of Dorchester's glories. They were laid out in the 18th century along the line of the Roman wall and bank, and enclose three sides of the town. Only a fragment of the Roman wall remains behind railings near Top o' Town.

The statue of William Barnes (1801-1886), the Dorset poet, outside the medieval church of St Peter's in the middle of Dorchester. Barnes was born near Sturminster Newton in the Blackmore Vale, but spent much of his life in or near Dorchester, first as owner of a small school, and from 1862 until his death as rector of Winterborne Came. Barnes is mainly remembered for his three volumes of Dorset dialect poetry, which as well as being a mine of information about rural life superbly evoke the preoccupations of Dorset working folk. Thomas Hardy knew Barnes well, and after his death recalled the aged clergyman, 'quaintly attired in caped cloak, knee breeches and buckled shoes, with a leather satchel slung over his shoulders, and a stout staff in his hand.' Barnes regularly visited Dorchester on market day, pausing near St Peter's to check his fob watch against the town clock. The statue is a fitting memorial, for as his biographer, Alan Chedzoy, has written, it is 'as if he had decided one market day not to go home, but had instead stepped up onto his plinth, so that the life of the county might continue to swirl about him.'

*Above* The Hardy Memorial at Top o' Town, Dorchester. Following Thomas Hardy's death in 1928 there were many suggestions for a fitting memorial, ranging from a statue on the heath to a huge tower. The final result was the life-size statue in Dorchester, sculpted by Eric Kennington and unveiled by Sir James Barrie (author of *Peter Pan* ) in September 1931.

*Right* The Cross and Hand, Batcombe Hill. The four feet high stone pillar stands in complete isolation on the verge of the ridge road between Minterne Magna and Evershot. Its purpose remains unclear, though it may well be a boundary mark. Thomas Hardy mentions it twice. In *Tess of the D'Urbervilles* Tess puts her hand on it mistakenly thinking it a cross and swears never to tempt Alec again by her 'charms or ways'. In his poem 'The Lost Pyx', Hardy tells the story of a priest being called out from Cerne Abbey to hear the confession of a man dying in a nearby cottage. The priest drops the sacrament on the journey. Retracing his steps, he finds it being protected by wild animals and lit by a beam of light. As a thanksgiving, he afterwards raises the stone, 'to mark where shone that midnight miracle.'

*Left* Looking North from Maiden Castle towards Middle Farm and the high chalk downland that fills much of the heart of the county.

*Below* The footings of the Roman temple on Maiden Castle. The immense 47 acre Iron Age hillfort is undoubtedly the most famous in Dorset, and is the only one to have been scientifically excavated. Part of it was first enclosed in about 3500 BC as a Neolithic camp. Later a remarkable long earthwork of 1790 feet, probably a bank barrow, was constructed across three-quarters of the fort. The Iron Age defences were started in about 350 BC, initially on a small scale, but by the date of the Roman attack in they had been extended to surround the entire hilltop in the form of three ramparts with elaborate entrances at the east and west. In AD 43 or 44 the 2nd Legion under the command of the future emperor Vespasian stormed the hillfort. In the 1930s the archaeologist Sir Mortimer Wheeler excavated part of the site. His finds were dramatic, for they included a war cemetery at the east gate in which 34 of the defenders had been buried, one with a Roman arrow-head embedded in his spine. The Roman temple dates to the fourth century AD. It was surrounded by a verandah, and had plastered walls coloured in panels of blue-green, dark red and white. A house for the priest stood close by.

The South Winterborne running alongside the village street in Winterborne St Martin (or Martinstown). The stream rises above Winterbourne Abbas and joins the Frome at West Stafford, passing through six of the fifteen Dorset villages prefixed by the name Winterborne. They only flow in winter, and according to tradition it is impossible to see a winter-borne break as they are dry one day and running the next. The villagers at Winterbourne Abbas once kept a watch on theirs for a fortnight. One night the watchman went to Bridehead Lodge to get a light for his pipe. Whilst away, the stream broke – unseen!

Judging rams at the May Dorchester Sheep Fair. There are about 135,000 sheep in the county, but the numbers were once much greater. Daniel Defoe claimed to see 600,000 within 6 miles of Dorchester in 1724. Many were Dorset Horn, a breed valued for its ability to lamb three times in two years. The county's other breeds are the hardier Dorset Down and the much rarer small-horned Portland. An old Dorset shearing song extolled the virtues of its flocks:

> *For their dung serves the corn ground*
> *And the wool clothes the poor;*
> *So drink up your liquor*
> *And fill up some more!*

Hang-glider pilots taking advantage of a break in the midwinter weather to fly from the top of Bell Hill out over the Blackmore Vale.

*Above* The House and Abbey Church, Milton Abbas. The great Benedectine Abbey was founded by King Athelstan in 934, and grew into one of the richest foundations in the West Country, with estates of more than 14,000 acres. The original building was destroyed by fire, and only the chancel, tower and transepts of its late-medieval replacement survive: the nave was never built.

Following the Dissolution of the Monasteries in 1539, the Abbey was bought by Sir John Tregonwell. Tregonwell's son, also called John, survived a fall from the top of the 60 feet Abbey tower at the age of five because the petticoats boys then wore acted as a parachute. In 1752 the estate was bought by Joseph Damer, who built Abbey House, the great mansion designed by Sir William

Chambers adjoining the Abbey, and which incorporates its original Great Hall. The House is now a school.

*Below left* The monument to Mary (Tregonwell) Banckes (1704), Jacob Banckes (1724), and John Banckes (1725) on the east wall of the north aisle, Milton Abbey.

*Opposite* The village street, Milton Abbas, with the almshouse of 1674. Until 1780 the town of Milton Abbas stood near the abbey church, but Joseph Damer (1718-1798), later Lord Milton, 1st Earl of Dorchester, disliked its proximity to his new house, and had the almshouse moved and all but one cottage on the edge of the town demolished. The new village originally consisted of 36 thatched cottages with plaster-faced brick walls. Each was designed for two families, and there was much overcrowding and poverty. Fanny Burney went there in 1791, and afterwards wrote: 'Every house was square and meant to resemble a gentlemen's abode; a very miserable mistake in his good Lordship . . . for the sight of the common people and of the poor labouring or strolling in and about these dwellings, made them appear rather to be reduced from better days than flourishing in a primitive or natural state.'

*Above* The upper reaches of the Cerne valley, with Minterne Parva on the left and Minterne Magna amongst the trees on the right.

*Right* The woodland garden at Minterne, Minterne Magna. Minterne was bought from the Churchills by Admiral Robert Digby in 1768 and is still owned by the family. 'Visited my new estate, valley very bare, trees not thriving', wrote the Admiral shortly after the purchase, an opinion completely at variance with the luxuriant garden that flourishes today. The Admiral planted the first trees and shrubs, as well as constructing the Elinor Bridge and a series of lakes. In 1880 the Hooker rhododendrons from the Himalayas started the collection for which Minterne is renowned. Seedlings from Tibet and China have also been planted, and though many of the specie rhododendrons are still unnamed it is said that at least one is in flower every day of the year.

taken by a messenger on horseback with the news that Lady Trenchard had committed suicide. At another dinner, on the day the Long Parliament began sitting in 1640, the sceptre fell from a carved figure of Charles II then in the Great Hall. The Long Parliament led to the Civil War, and ultimately to Charles II's execution. More cheerfully, a carriage can still be heard rattling up the stairs as a reminder of the Trenchard who successfully wagered that he could drive a horse and carriage up the great stone staircase.

*Opposite below* The Tudor manor house of Athelhampton, near Puddletown. The house was started in 1493 by Sir William Martyn, Lord Mayor of London, and was continued by his descendants through the 16th century. The oriel window (to the left of the two storey porch) and the Great Hall were both built by Sir William. The window still contains fragments of its original heraldic glass, and the fine timber roof of the hall is also original. Sadly, the early Tudor gatehouse was demolished in 1862, but by way of compensation the gardens are gorgeous. Many are contained in walled courts, and they include clipped yew pyramids, lily ponds and fountains, as well as a wild garden and a succession of walks.

*Top* Looking out over Upper Sydling and the head of the Sydling valley.

*Above* Early morning in Sydling St Nicholas, with both the milkman and postman doing their rounds.

*Opposite above* Wolfeton, Charminster, the home of the Trenchards from 1480 until late in the 18th century. The earliest parts of the house, which include the gatehouse and stair tower, date from about 1500. No other Dorset house has inspired so many tales of ghosts and hauntings. A judge who went to Wolfeton to dine during the 17th century supposedly saw the figure of Lady Trenchard standing behind her chair, with her throat cut and holding her head under her arm. He abruptly ordered his carriage and left, only to be over-

Cerne Abbas from the lower slopes of Giant Hill, with the Abbot's Hall visible amongst the trees on the right. It seems probable that many of the buildings of the great Benedictine abbey at Cerne stood in the field close to the wall, though no trace remains. According to legend, St Augustine visited Cerne and created the spring feeding St Augustine's Well by plunging his staff into the ground. The original Saxon monastery in the village was refounded in 987 by Ethelmaer, Earl of Cornwall, and dissolved in 1539. At its height, it was one of Dorset's wealthiest abbeys, with possessions scattered throughout the county. The last abbot, Thomas Corton (who was born at Corton, near Portesham), was accused of allowing the handful of monks still there at the Dissolution to play cards and celebrate the Mass without washing, as well as himself cohabiting with five different women, and using Abbey funds for the benefit of his illegitimate children.

*Left* The Abbot's Hall, Cerne Abbas, showing the elaborate two-storey oriel window above the entrance. The name is misleading, for in fact it is the porch that once led into the hall, and was built by Abbot Thomas Sam (1497-1509) as part of a range of private lodgings that included a chapel, kitchen and library.

*Above* Timber-framed houses in Abbey Street, Cerne Abbas, built in about 1500. In 1814, to celebrate a temporary truce with France during the Napoleonic Wars, 400 villagers sat down to roast beef and plum pudding at a 255 feet long line of tables placed in the middle of the street. A triumphal arch decorated with laurel was built at each end, whose centrepiece was a hogshead of beer (or five pints per person). Cerne Abbas was well-known for its beers, and for the quantity downed in its 14 inns. 'Vice and immorality abounded on every hand,' wrote a new minister in 1812. 'The Sabbath was universally profaned, being used for pleasure, business and getting drunk'. Smuggling was also widespread, and one 18th century wag reckoned you could walk the length of Long Street without ever having to step on anything other than kegs of brandy.

# THE PIDDLE AND FROME
# VALLEYS

# THE PIDDLE AND FROME
# VALLEYS

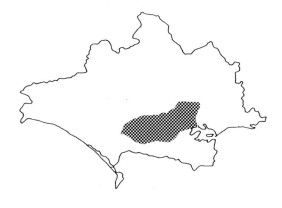

Few landscapes more dominate a novel than the area of heath and river valley to the east of Dorchester. For this is the Egdon Heath of Thomas Hardy's *Return of the Native*. Hardy was born in a cottage on its western rim in 1840, and today his birthplace is amongst the most visited places in Dorset.

In Hardy's day much of the heath was virtual wilderness inhabited by small ponies and furze-gatherers. The heath drains into the rivers Piddle and Frome, forming a landscape he described as 'majestic without severity, impressive without showiness, emphatic in its admonitions, grand in its simplicity'. And yet the apparent simplicity masks endless minor changes. Water meadows border the edge of the chalk between Puddletown and Turner's Puddle. Elsewhere there are forestry plantations, watercress beds, areas where wild rhododendrons have swept aside the gorse, steep hollows like Culpepper's Dish where the acid waters of the heath have eaten into the chalk. The true heath is perhaps best seen either side of the road between Bere Regis and Wool, though much of it is reserved for tank training.

*Previous page* Water Crowfoot in flower on the River Piddle near Puddletown.

*Left* The interior of the tiny 12th century church of St Andrew, Winterborne Tomson, and quite simply one of the most beautiful churches in Dorset. The church was fitted with its lovely rustic box pews, pulpit and gallery in about 1720, but for a long time lay derelict. In 1930 it was carefully restored by the architect A.R. Powys, brother of the writers John Cowper, Llewelyn and T.F. Powys, with the proceeds from the sale of Thomas Hardy's correspondence with the Society for the Protection of Ancient Buildings.

The upstairs bedroom in which Thomas Hardy was born in 1840, and in which he wrote his first five books, including *Under the Greenwood Tree* (1872) and *Far from the Madding Crowd* (1874).

The cottage at Higher Bockhampton in which Thomas Hardy was born in 1840, three miles from Dorchester. By any estimation Hardy is one of the greatest of English writers, and much of what he wrote is set in his native county, often drawing on stories told to him by his grandmother and mother. Hardy's father was a mason and builder, and the cottage was built in 1801 by Hardy's great-grandfather for his grandparents in what was then a wild landscape of uncultivated woodland and heath. Hardy's family lived in the cottage until 1912, and in 1948 it was acquired by the National Trust. Describing it in his earliest surviving poem, he wrote:

*Our house stood quite alone, and those tall firs*
*And beeches were not planted. Snakes and efts* *
*Swarmed in the summer days, and nightly bats*
*Would fly about our bedrooms. Heathcroppers* **
*Lived on the hills, and were our only friends;*
*So wild it was when first we settled here.*
* newts  ** ponies

Other cottages as well as Hardy's enjoy literary links. William Barnes, the Dorset poet, lived in the thatched rectory near Winterborne Came and is buried in its churchyard. T.E.Lawrence (of Arabia) spent the last years of his life in the tiny cottage of Cloud's Hill, and is buried at Moreton. Each has its visitors, but the most crowded village in July is Tolpuddle, which annually hosts a Trades Union rally in memory of the Tolpuddle Martyrs – six farmworkers who in 1834 were transported to Australia for illegally administering an oath in an attempt to form a trades union.

Bere Regis and Wool are the area's largest villages, whilst its houses include the medieval fortified manor of Woodsford Castle, the classical Came House, and Charborough Park, which is best known for its tower and the stag and lion on the entrance gates set into the brick wall along the Dorchester/Wimborne road.

The area also boasts three of Dorset's loveliest churches. The most northerly is the tiny 12th century church at Winterborne Tomson, with its box pews and gallery. Bere Regis is renowned for its carved stone faces with tooth and head-aches, and for the huge carved figures of the Apostles looking down into the nave from the roof. Moreton is different again, and no one should pass by without pausing to look at the glorious engraved glass that fills every window. The effect is magical, and a complete contrast to the surrounding heath.

Evening light on a meander on the River Frome near Holmebridge.

Watercress beds at Silver Springs Watercress farm in the Frome valley near Moreton. Dorset has long been known for its watercress, which is mainly grown in the pure mineral-rich water of the chalk streams, where artesian wells provide a plentiful supply of water at a constant temperature. Today there about 47 acres of beds in the county.

Woolbridge Manor, Wool, and the 16th century Woolbridge over the Frome. Thanks to Thomas Hardy, and its setting on the water meadows, the early 17th century manor house is amongst the best known of all Dorset houses, for it is where Tess and Angel Clare spent their unhappy honeymoon in *Tess of the D'Urbervilles*. Hardy's choice of house was deliberate, for it had once belonged to the ancient Dorset family of Turberville, of whom he made Tess a humble descendant. The Turbervilles finally died out early in the 18th century, when the twin daughters of the last male Turberville died on the same day in the same house.

Whitcombe church, given by King Athelstan to Milton Abbey and now redundant. One wall of the nave and a doorway are 12th century, but of most interest internally are the wall paintings showing St Christopher wading through water with Christ as a child on his shoulders and a mermaid combing her hair in a mirror.

The west front of Moreton House, built in 1744 in Portland stone by James Frampton (died 1784), whose memorial is the obelisk to the south-east on Fir Hill and whose family had owned the manor since the 14th century.

*Below left* The Trinity Chapel window, St Nicholas Church, Moreton, engraved by Laurence Whistler in 1982 as a memorial to a pilot shot down in the Battle of Britain. The medieval church was burnt down in 1776 and replaced by the present Georgian building. In 1940 a bomb destroyed the glass, and between 1955 and 1984 Laurence Whistler engraved all twelve windows in the church, choosing light as his theme. Salisbury Cathedral, near where the pilot was stationed, is visible at the foot of the centre panel, with the English and French coasts in the background.

*Below* Cloud's Hill, T.E.Lawrence's cottage near Bovington Camp which now belongs to the National Trust. To escape his fame as Lawrence of Arabia, Lawrence joined the Tank Corps in 1923, and was living at Cloud's Hill at the time of his fatal motorbike accident in 1935. Describing the cottage, he once wrote: '. . . it is alone in a dip in the moor, very quiet, very lonely, very bare. A mile from camp. Furnished with a bed, a bicycle, three chairs, 100 books, a gramophone of parts, a table. Many windows, oak trees, an ilex, Birch, firs, rhododendron, laurels, heather, Dorsetshire to look at.' It was where he prepared *Seven Pillars of Wisdom* for publication. The words 'Why worry?' are inscribed over the entrance in Greek.

The entrance to Bladen Hill, Briantspuddle, with the War Memorial by Eric Gill. In 1914 the wealthy London draper Sir Ernest Debenham bought land and farms in the area with the idea of creating a model estate. After the First World War farm buildings and cottages were built in the 'Arts and Crafts' style, using locally-made concrete blocks and bricks. Traditional cob walls were also built, many of the cottages were thatched. Piped water and electricity were laid on from the pump and power house in the centre of the village. There was a Central Milk Factory and dairy farm with stalls for 100 cows. Sir Ernest regarded the estate as an attempt to prove that Great Britain could feed itself, and its activities included forestry, bee-keeping, a chicken farm, pedigree stock raising and a veterinary service. Following his death in 1952 the estate was broken up and sold.

The thatched shelter erected by Sir Ernest Debenham in 1934 on the centenary of the trial of the Tolpuddle Martyrs. The stump of the sycamore on the left is all that remains of the tree under which the Martyrs used to meet. The six Martyrs were George and James Loveless, James Hammett, Thomas and John Standfield, and James Brine. In 1833, faced with a decline in the agricultural wage from ten shillings (50p) a week to seven shillings (35p), the six labourers, five of whom were Methodists, set up a tiny – and legal – agricultural union as a way of bringing pressure to bear on the local landowners. At its formation they took a pledge of loyalty, and it was that for which they were arrested. The Unlawful Oaths Act had been passed in 1797 to deal with a naval mutiny, but never repealed. As a result, the six men were found guilty and sentenced to seven years' transportation. There was a national outcry, and three years later the men were granted a free pardon. Only James Hammett returned to Tolpuddle, the rest settled in Canada, but all six men are remembered in the village: by the Memorial seat, the arch to the Methodist Chapel, and the six Memorial cottages built by the TUC in 1934.

Woodsford Castle. The Castle, which stands close to the River Frome west of Dorchester, was originally built as a fortified manor house in about 1337 when William de Whitefield was given permission to crenellate his house at 'Wyrdesford'. By 1630 it was 'allmost ruinated', and during the 18th century it was converted into a thatched farmhouse. It now belongs to the Landmark Trust.

The Stag Gate, Charborough Park – a familiar sight alongside the A31 between Wimborne and Bere Regis. Both the Stag Gate, and the Lion Gate, as well as the long brick wall that runs alongside the road, were built in 1841-1842 after the owner of Charborough Park, J.S.W. Sawbridge Erle Drax, had successfully had the new Wimborne/Dorchester turnpike moved further away from his house. More than two million bricks were used in the wall, but unfortunately for Sawbridge Erle Drax – who was also its chief promoter – the turnpike lost money, mainly because the railway between Wimborne and Dorchester opened shortly afterwards. In the centre of the Park is Charborough House, which incorporates parts of the house built by the commander of the Parliamentary forces that besieged Corfe Castle, Sir Walter Erle (stone and timber taken from Corfe Castle were used in the building). The House has been owned by the same family since Elizabethan times, and their surname is now Plunkett-Ernle-Erle-Drax.

# THE ISLE OF PURBECK

# THE ISLE OF PURBECK

Purbeck is really a peninsula, not an island, for as Thomas Gerard wrote in 1622 it can be entered without crossing 'anie water at all'. Yet most visitors do cross water, either at Wareham over the tidal Frome or eastward where the river narrows. But from whichever direction you approach, the Purbeck Hills rise up ahead to provide the clue to Purbeck's name. The 'pur' comes from the Old English for a snipe or bittern, whose beak or 'beck' the chalk ridge resembles. As well as being referred to as an island, the words 'forest' and 'warren' were also used to describe Purbeck. For it was once a royal hunting preserve whose deer were hunted by the medieval kings.

Between Wareham and the hills, as well as east to Studland, is mostly heath. There are ball-clay workings, forestry plantations, and – most recently – the wells and storage tanks of Britain's largest onshore oilfield at Wytch Farm. The list does the heath less than justice. Studland's beaches are sandy and sheltered. Creeks and mud flats stretch along Poole Harbour. Much of the Arne peninsula is a Nature Reserve, home to deer, orchids, and adders, as well as over-wintering waders and heathland birds.

The hills divide the heath from the rest of Purbeck. Beginning at Old Harry's chalk stack off Handfast Point, they drive westward as a thin ridge that gradually widens behind Lulworth Cove and Durdle Door. The views from their summits are superb: over the heath and Poole Harbour, out over Wareham behind its Saxon ramparts, and – most famously – towards Corfe Castle atop its knoll on the only gap in the ridge.

Corfe's summer crowds give way to farmland that reaches east to the resort town of Swanage and west to Tyneham, the abandoned village evacuated in 1943 for use by the Army and now in the centre of their firing ranges. Neolithic settlers first farmed the area, and successive generations have added to their legacy. Old Saxon trackways link small manor houses and deserted medieval hamlets. Copses and spinneys fringe ancient hedges.

The rich green of the Wealden valley could not be in greater contrast than with the land running south to the sea. Here Purbeck's geology becomes a mixture of limestones, shale and clay whose origins date back millions of years. Fossilised dinosaur footprints have been found, as well as marsh crocodiles, turtles and primitive mammals. Iron Age craftsmen fashioned bangles and spindlewhorls from the Kimmeridge Shale. But it is the limestone quarries that scar the windswept coastal plateau that have yielded Purbeck's most enduring harvest. Purbeck marble was first quarried by the Romans, and during the Middle Ages a constant supply left Purbeck every year to decorate churches all over England. The limestone beds were worked for building stone, roofing slates and the many dry-stone walls that still divide the fields. Old quarry workings are everywhere, and can be seen best on the coast, where as an added bonus the cliff path running the length of Purbeck allows a series of glorious walks.

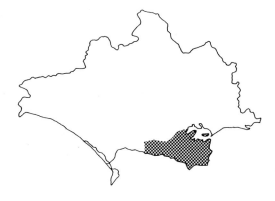

*Previous page* Walkers on Ballard Down.

*Opposite* Looking east over Durdle Door, towards St Oswald's Bay, Dungy Head and Lulworth. Durdle Door's name is derived from the Old English for 'pierced'.

*Below* The most famous bay on the Dorset coast, Lulworth Cove. The cove was formed when the sea broke through the hard Portland limestone cliff, eroding out the softer sands and clays and forming a 350 feet high chalk cliff at the back. Its waters are supposedly the coldest in Dorset, partly because of their depth, partly because the cove is fed by small springs at the foot of the cliff.

Wareham Quay and the River Frome. Wareham sits between two rivers, the Piddle and the Frome, and the latter is still tidal at the bridge, despite being twelve miles from the open sea. Wareham's history has been turbulent, and more full of set-backs than most Dorset towns. The Saxons built its defences, the Vikings pillaged, King Stephen besieged it during the Anarchy (1139-1154), and by the end of the Civil War it had changed hands four times. Following Monmouth's Rebellion of 1685 some of his supporters were hung, drawn and quartered on the Bloody Bank on the Saxon ramparts. Fires of 1704 and 1742 were followed by the blaze of 1762 in which 133 houses were destroyed after some red hot ashes on a dunghill were fanned into flame by the wind. Poole's rise and the gradual silting of the Frome may have ended Wareham's days as a port, but it is still the gateway to Purbeck. In summer it fills with visitors. Small boats line the Quay or lie at the moorings in the river.

Upstream on the River Frome from Redcliffe Farm with the tower of St Mary's church, Wareham, in the background.

The full length marble statue of T.E.Lawrence (1888-1935) by Eric Kennington in St Martin's, Wareham. Lawrence is dressed in Arab robes, his head on a camel saddle and one hand holding a curved dagger. He died near Bovington in a motor-bike accident and is buried at Moreton.

East Street, Wareham. Away from the traffic on South and North Streets Wareham remains un-spoilt and unhurried. Much of the town was destroyed in the fire of 1762 and so there is a rich mixture of late 18th and early 19th century buildings. East Street is the home of the weekly market, the Museum, and the Georgian Streche's Almshouses, originally endowed for the 'main-tenance of six antient Men and five Women' in 1418, and rebuilt in 1741.

St Martin's, Wareham, the only Saxon church in Dorset to largely survive in its original form. The present church dates from 1042, but was preceded by one supposedly founded in 698 by St Aldhelm whilst waiting for a change of wind before crossing to France. It was here that a West Saxon king was buried after being mistakenly poisoned by his wife. Amongst the fragments of wall paintings inside is one showing St Martin sharing his cloak with a beggar.

Corfe Castle from Corfe Common. The parallel
lines visible crossing the Common are the remains
of the medieval hollow-ways leading into Corfe,
along which horse-drawn sledges carried marble
and freestone from the Purbeck quarries to be
worked by masons in the town. Corfe Castle is
Dorset's most famous landmark – and its most
visited: about 160,000 visitors annually enter the
gateway and climb the slopes of the natural mound
on which the Castle is built. Nothing remains of
the Saxon building near which Edward the Martyr
was murdered at the order of his step-mother in
978, but it is possible that it stood in the West
Bailey. William the Conqueror began the surviving
Castle's construction shortly after the Norman
invasion, and it was strengthened and added to
throughout the Middle Ages. The two ruined walls
rising from the hilltop were part of the 13th century Keep, which contained the King's Hall and
the royal apartments. The Castle was never a
permanent royal residence, but its strategic importance on the only gap in the Purbeck Hills was
significant, and monarchs stayed in it when travelling round the kingdom. The most famous episode
in its history took place during the Civil War when
it was held for the king by Lady Bankes, wife of its
owner. With a garrison of only five men and a
handful of maids 'Brave Dame Mary' resisted a
siege in 1643, only to be forced to surrender three
years later when treachery allowed Parliamentary
forces to enter the Castle disguised as reinforce-
ments. The Castle was looted, its walls pulled
down and its towers blown up, leaving the ruin
that endures today.

*Above* Autumn sunlight on Hartland Moor. The Moor is a National Nature Reserve and deliberately managed so that the bell heather and Dorset heath continue to flourish amidst the peat bogs. Nightjars can be heard from sunset onwards during the summer. Dorset's first railway once ran across part of the Moor. Called Frayle's Tramway, it was named after a London potter who built it in 1806 to transport ball-clay from the open-cast workings at Norden to a quay at Middlebere on the edge of Poole Harbour. Brimstone butterflies now thrive amongst the buckthorn either side of the abandoned track, along which teams of horses once pulled five two-ton wagons.

Corfe Castle from the south-west, with visitors enjoying the sunshine outside the Greyhound Hotel in the Market Place.

The Agglestone on Godlingston Heath, with the Little Sea and Studland Bay in the background. The 500 ton block of sandstone was supposedly thrown by the Devil from the Isle of Wight at Corfe Castle in a moment of irritation. It fell short, and remains 'a monument of disappointed malice, a wonder to the peasantry, and a theme of antiquarian conjecture.'

The Pinnacles and Handfast Point from Ballard
Down, with the Bournemouth skyline in the
background. The coast walk from Swanage is
superb, with wild flowers along the cliff-top,
cormorants, and plenty of boats rounding the
headland in summer. The cliffs rise to 200 feet at
their highest, with a series of caves at their base.
The biggest, Parson's Barn, which is 40 feet high,
was a smuggler's hiding-place, and was where
Customs officers found a cargo of tea in 1747. An
attempt by the smugglers to retrieve it from Poole
Customs House led to the death of two officers,
and the subsequent hanging of six of the gang. It
was along this stretch of coast that a ship carrying
bells for St James's, Poole, is supposed to have
sunk as punishment for the blasphemy of its crew:
the bells still toll from the sea bed in storms.

An aerial view of the BP Gathering Station at Wytch Farm, with Poole Harbour in the background. The Gathering Station forms the heart of the oilfield, and is where the oil, water and gas produced from the nine wellsites are separated and treated. Oil in workable quantities was first discovered in 1974, and production began five years later. Wytch Farm is the largest onshore oilfield in Western Europe, with reserves of 10,000 million gallons. Current production is 60,000 barrels a day, which is exported via a 56 mile pipeline to a terminal at Hamble on Southampton Water.

Great Western railway class '56xx' 0-6-2T No 5619 approaching Harman's Cross. The railway to Swanage closed in 1972 but the five miles of track to Corfe Castle has since been relaid by the Swanage Railway Company. No 5619 was built in 1925, and after a spell at Paddington spent the rest of its working life in the Welsh valleys, to be finally rescued from a scrapyard in 1976 and restored.

*Below* The mill pond, Church Hill, Swanage. Until the arrival of the railway in 1885 Swanage was a small stone-shipping and fishing port with pretensions to being a resort. The mill house at the bottom of Church Hill dates to 1734, but there is no trace of the bakery, forge and small school that once faced the pond.

*Below right* The 40 ton Portland stone Globe at Durlston Country Park, Swanage. Durlston owes its existence to the formidable – and eccentric (though he would have hated being described as such) – stone and building contractor George Burt (1816-1894). He and his Weymouth architect, G.R. Crickmay, built the nearby Castle in 1887-8 as a deliberate fake for use as a restuarant. All over the Country Park there are stone benches and plaques set up by Burt giving information or improving quotations. The Globe is surrounded by slabs inscribed with Shakespearean or Biblical passages, whilst others remain blank for intending graffiti artists: 'Persons anxious to write their names will do so on this stone only.' The 260 acre Park is now run by Dorset County Council, with a visitor centre on quarrying and wildlife.

*Right* The Wellington Clock Tower from near Peveril Point, with Swanage sea-front in the background. Architecturally, Swanage is dominated by the scavengings of John Mowlem (1788-1868) and his nephew George Burt (1816-1894), the stone and building contractors. The Clock Tower was first erected at one end of London Bridge in 1854 as a memorial to the Duke of Wellington. Other London relics include the front of the Town Hall, originally the facade of the Mercer's Hall in Cheapside, built in 1670 after the Great Fire of London, and the cast iron lamp standards on The Parade and Beach Road, which came from Hanover Square. Most remarkable of all is Purbeck House, George Burt's house in the High Street, which is built from chippings from the Albert Memorial, and incorporates a bollard from Millbank Prison, an archway from Hyde Park Corner, some cast iron columns from Billingsgate Market, as well as a mosaic and floor tiles from the Palace of Westminster.

Cottages at Worth Matravers, built from stone taken from the Old Quarry at Winspit. Worth was traditionally one of the main centres of the quarrying industry, and old quarry workings scar the surrounding limestone plateau. London Row remains a link with the city to which much of its stone was sent, whilst the tools used to prepare it for cutting gave their name to the Square and Compass pub. A headstone in the graveyard of St Nicholas Church marks the burial place of Benjamin Jesty, who in 1774 became the first person to inoculate against smallpox by inoculating his wife and family with the milder cow pox using a stocking needle.

St Aldhelm's Chapel, St Aldhelm's Head. The original purpose of the Norman chapel remains unclear, though we know it was served by a royal chaplain during the 13th century. The lack of fact has embroidered the fiction. One legend ascribes its construction to a local squire who after watching his daughter and her bridegroom set sail then witnessed their drowning in the notorious race off the Head. He afterwards paid for the Chapel as a chantry where masses could be sung for the drowned and whose roof could support a warning beacon. On Whit Tuesday, Worth fair day, the villagers decorated the Chapel with blossom and danced round its paved floor.

Smedmore House, Kimmeridge. The manor was bought by William Wyot from the de Smedmores in 1391 and has remained associated with the Wyot family ever since, passing either through marriage or inheritance to first the Clavells and then the Mansels, who still live in it today. The bow-fronted Georgian facade conceals the remains of the original house of about 1620, which was built by Sir William Clavell, a picturesque adventurer who nearly bankrupted himself, first by trying to extract alum from the nearby cliffs, and secondly by setting up a glass works fuelled by Kimmeridge shale. The result was losses of £20,000 and a place in Marshalsea debtors prison. When a descendant, John Clavell, left Smedmore to his niece after dying childless in 1833, his servants, led by the housekeeper, forged a will stating that it had been left to them – a view not shared by the courts. The lovely gardens are largely the creation of Major and Mrs John Mansel over the last forty years.

The ruined Clavell Tower on Hen Cliff overlooking Kimmeridge Bay. The tower was built in 1831 by the Reverend John Richards, who had inherited Smedmore in 1817 and changed his name to Clavell, and for a while it was used as a coastguard's look-out. The cliff beneath is formed of the Kimmeridge shales used by Sir William Clavell in the 17th century in the alum works and glass factory that all but bankrupted him. The alum was extracted from the shale for use as fuel, but, as a contemporary wrote, 'in burneing yeelds such an offensive Savour and extraordinarie Blacknesse, that the people labouring about these Fires are more like Furies than Men.' All attempts to exploit the shale enjoyed a similar fate, but perhaps the most ambitious – and foolhardy – was the company formed in 1858 to light Paris using Kimmeridge gas.

Creech Grange. The estate was originally a grange or granary of Bindon Abbey, near Wool. Following the Dissolution of the Monasteries it was bought by Sir Oliver Lawrence, brother-in-law of Henry VIII's Lord Chancellor. Only fragments remain of the house built by Lawrence before his death in 1559, partly because it was damaged by fire by the Parliamentarians during the Civil War, and finally because in 1846 the entire front was taken down and rebuilt in the local Tudor style. In 1691 the house and estate was bought by the Bond family, one of whom lost a fortune laying out the London street that bears his name.

Blackmanston Farm, Steeple. The Kimmeridge Clay vale either side of the tiny Corfe River has always provided some of the richest dairy pasture in Dorset. Blackmanston Farm was originally built as a Elizabethan manor house, but the stone footings of a Saxon settlement have been found nearby.

The deserted village of Tyneham, with the medieval church of St Mary in the background. In 1943 the entire village was evacuated, and it now forms the centre of a 7,500 acre Army firing range. When the villagers left they pinned a note to the church door: 'Please treat the church and houses with care; we have given up our homes where many of us lived for generations to help win the war to keep men free. We shall return one day and thank you for treating the village kindly.' The Government went back on its promise to give the village back and in 1948 it was compulsorily purchased by the Army. Shelling, neglect and vandalism have all but destroyed it. Despite the conversion of both the school and church into museums, and the thriving wildlife on the surrounding ranges, an air of sadness haunts the village and its roofless cottages.

The village of Corfe Castle and the church of St Edward, King and Martyr. The building on the left in the Market Place with the projecting bay is Town House, with the Mayor's Robing Room on the first floor. Corfe was granted charters by Saxon kings, but grew to prominence in the shadow of the Castle. Most of the best buildings date to the late 16th and early 17th centuries, when the town was at its most prosperous. The Castle's destruction gradually led to Corfe's decline, and the 18th century historian, John Hutchins, thought 'the appearance of misery in the town is only too striking'. Until the Reform Act of 1832 it was a Rotten Borough, with two MPs. Bribery was common, with votes being bought with money and beer.

# STONE QUARRYING

Dorset's building materials vary immensely, but the one unifying material is stone, which in some places has been quarried since Roman times, and which still endures in buildings the length of the county. The Heath-stone from which the Norman masons built Wimborne's minster is no longer quarried, nor is the Green-sand that shaped Shaftesbury. The hundreds of small limestone quarries scattered across the north and west are now overgrown and abandoned, but to them we owe the medieval manor of Fiddleford, Abbotsbury's great tithe barn, as well as churches, cottages and farmhouses in virtually every Dorset parish.

Yet there are two places where stone is still quarried, and the words written about Portland by John Claridge in 1793 remain true today. 'As to quarries, the whole island of

*Above* Members of the Ancient Order of Marblers and Stonecutters following their annual Shrove Tuesday meeting in Corfe Castle Town Hall. After gathering in the Fox Inn, the quarriers make their progress to Ower Quay, across the heath on the edge of Poole Harbour, kicking a football and carrying a pound of pepper as payment for their ancient right to ship stone from the Quay. Ower was the main medieval port for the export of Purbeck limestone and marble. Much of it was dressed in Corfe and then hauled to Ower along now overgrown and abandoned hollow-ways. The stone was then transferred to flat-bottomed barges which were rowed out to the waiting cargo ships in South Deep.

*Left* The old quarry workings at Winspit, close to the coast south of Worth Matravers.

Portland seems to be one mass of the most beautiful stone, chiefly used in the metropolis and elsewhere for the most superb buildings, and universally admired for its close texture and durability, surpassing any other.'

The Island of Portland is a solid block of limestone, and the earliest quarries were dug close to the cliff face. Once the stone had been split from its bed with wedges, it was tumbled onto the Weares below, where the stone was roughly cut and dragged on sledges to the shipping piers. By 1600, when one visitor found Portland 'all full of works and quarries of stone', the dressed stone had been used locally for Rufus and Portland Castles, as well as Christchurch Priory and the Palace of Westminster.

The biggest impetus to the industry followed Christopher Wren's decision to rebuild St Paul's Cathedral in Portland stone following the Great Fire of London in 1666. By the time of its completion, and fifty other London churches, nearly six million tons had been shipped by barge from Portland to the capital. Portlanders visiting London today are surrounded by stone quarried by their forefathers: the Law Courts, Somerset House, Regent Street, the British and Victoria and Albert Museums, the Admiralty building and Cenotaph in Whitehall. Some calculate that there is more Portland stone in London than left unquarried in Dorset.

The other great quarrying area is also an island only in name, and the stone harvested from it is another hard limestone, known – confusingly – as Purbeck-Portland. Most of the freestone quarries in Purbeck are concentrated on the bleak plateau between Swanage and Saint Aldhelm's Head, and have been worked for local use since the Middle Ages. Some, like Tilly Whim and Winspit, were close to the cliff, and now survive as a honeycomb of tunnels and caverns from where the stone was taken to be lowered to the barges below.

Purbeck's most famous stone is Purbeck marble, which isn't a true marble, but a hard limestone crowded with the small shells of the freshwater pond-snail. It is found in two seams, never more than four feet thick, that run between Worbarrow and Peveril Point. It is usually bluish-grey, but can have a reddish or greenish tint, and owes its name to its ability to take polish.

Purbeck marble was certainly quarried by the Romans. When the wife and children of a Roman who had died in Dorchester selected a tombstone, they chose Purbeck marble. But its heyday was the Middle Ages, when it was widely used for decoration. From the quarries it went to Corfe Castle, to be worked by masons and marblers, then on by cart to the stone-ports lining Poole Harbour. Much of it ended its days in churches – as fonts, altar tables, floor-slabs, effigies and shafts. One woman gave Salisbury Cathedral its polished piers as a gift from her Dunshay quarries.

Happily, Purbeck marble is still being quarried, all be it in smaller quantities. The same is true of the freestone, both in Purbeck and on Portland. For a while it seemed that concrete might make real stone redundant, but nothing can compete with finely carved stone worked by a skilled mason with his chisels, and its use is on the increase, both for restoration work and new buildings.

Two contrasts in drilling.

*Top* A pneumatic drill at work at W. J. Haysom's Quarry in Purbeck. The holes are drilled about five feet apart, and finally packed with black powder, so as to free the stone from its bed.

*Bottom* A high speed drilling machine at Coombefield Quarry, Portland. The drill is operated electronically, and can drill seven feet in forty seconds.

*Above* Trimming stone at Coombefield Quarry.

*Left* The ARC South Western Coombefield Quarry on Portland. About 10,000 cubic metres of building stone are quarried annually, and ARC will soon be opening up a new face to provide the stone needed for the rebuilding of Paternoster Square, near St Paul's Cathedral.

*Below* Peter Worrall of Easton Masonry, Portland, using an air gun to rough out the background of a carving for Vintner's Place, London, prior to hand-carving. Easton Masonry have recently completed some restoration work for Buckingham Palace, as well as the new Sainsbury Wing of the National Gallery.

*Above* The interior of the main masonry building at W. J. Haysom's Quarry near St Aldhelm's Head. Most of the Purbeck-Portland limestone taken from the quarry is used for building work, and recently the company supplied the stone for completing Portsmouth Cathedral, a task first started in the 1930s using stone from the same quarry. Purbeck limestone splits well into paving, and paving cut at Haysom's was used for the restoration work at Hampton Court.

# POOLE HARBOUR
# BOURNEMOUTH AND
# THE EAST

# POOLE HARBOUR
# BOURNEMOUTH AND THE EAST

In 1805 Edward Brayley wrote, 'the greatest part of this is most dreary waste, serving only in the summer to support a few ordinary sheep and cattle, and to supply the neighbouring villages with firing.' No houses then stood within three miles of the mouth of the Bourne. There was a decoy hut for wildfowlers, but otherwise travellers between Poole and Christchurch crossed empty heathland divided by narrow chines leading down to beaches where smuggling gangs landed their cargoes.

That same year much of the land now occupied by Bournemouth was enclosed, divided and sold. Plantations of pine were planted, an inn opened close to the Bourne. Five years later, Lewis Tregonwell, a Captain in the Dorset Rifle Volunteers, gave in to the wishes of his wife and paid £179 for 8½ acres near the river mouth. On it he built a cottage for his butler and a mansion for himself, the remains of which are now encased in the Royal Exeter Hotel. Bournemouth had been born. By the 1840s it was being touted as the 'very first invalid sea-watering place in England'. In 1870 the railway arrived, and the town's population accelerated: 17,000 in 1880, 60,000 by the turn of the century, 150,000 by 1990.

Bournemouth's inland march over the heath, and its wholesale swallowing of the villages standing in its way, was limited by the towns to its east and west, and their still unspoilt harbours. Christchurch grew up where the Avon and Stour meet. The small Saxon settlement acquired a Norman castle and a priory. The harbour entrance is guarded by Hengistbury Head, once a busy Iron Age port and now a Nature Reserve.

Poole Harbour is altogether on a quite different scale. Ninety miles of coastline enclose a scattering of islands, 10,000 acres of water and a hundred miles of navigable channels. Virtually all of it is a delight, despite being crowded throughout the summer with bathers, wind-surfers, cross-Channel ferries, fishermen, and every form of craft imaginable – from gin palaces to sailing dinghies.

Poole's fortunes are inevitably linked to its site. By the 15th century the wool trade had made it the largest port between Southampton and Exeter. Decline was followed by the growth of trade with Newfoundland, which filled its warehouses with cod, oil, furs and sealskins. Bournemouth's birth halted a second decline, and, despite suffering the worst excesses of post-war planning, Poole is now Dorset's largest town.

Wimborne lies inland from Poole on the far side of the heath. It grew up round a monastery founded by a king of Wessex in the 8th century, and is today a bustling market town dominated by the twin towers of the minster. The open heath to Wimborne's north-east has finally been reached by the brick and concrete ripples spreading inland from the coast, and the eastern heath is now the most threatened area in the county.

*Previous page* Brownsea Castle, Brownsea Island, with the Family Pier built by Colonel Waugh in the mid 19th century on the right. Colonel Waugh is just one of the owners who have contributed to the Island's colourful history. After refacing the Castle, rebuilding the church and starting a pottery producing sewage and drainage pipes, he went bankrupt in 1857. His wife must share the blame. When members of Poole's Corporation landed intending to ask the Colonel to stand for Parliament, she mistakenly thought they were creditors asking for payment and said 'Only give us time and we will pay.' The Castle stands where Henry VIII built a fortified blockhouse in 1547. In the 18th century it was turned into an imitation castle which burnt down in 1898. After being rebuilt, it was bought by the reclusive Mrs Bonham Christie, who allowed the Island to become a wilderness. Since 1961 it has belonged to the National Trust.

The Bournemouth skyline from Branksome Chine, showing the Pier, which incorporates a theatre, restaurants, a discotheque and amusement arcades. The town's piers have had a chequered history. The first, of 1856, suffered storm damage and was replaced within five years. The second, of timber and 1000 feet long, was unsafe by 1877, by which time the pierhead had been swept away, gales had reduced its length and shipworm had weakened the piles. The present pier dates to 1880, though much of it had to be rebuilt following the Second World War after the neck had been blown up to prevent the Germans using it to land invasion troops.

Air traffic controllers at work inside the Control Tower at Bournemouth International Airport, Hurn. The Airport was opened in 1941 and was used for paratroop training and as a glider base before the North African Landings in 1943. Prior to D Day, it was the base of 570 Squadron, who landed agents and dropped supplies to the French Resistance. In the wake of the Normandy Landings it was base to 84 Group, nine squadrons of Typhoons, who flew daily to France and mounted their attacks from improvised front-line airstrips. Between November 1944 and the opening of Heathrow in January 1946 it was the main land terminal for BOAC, and starting point of the first England-Australia service, which took three days in modified Lancaster bombers. It is now a regional airport, flying scheduled services to the Channel Islands and British cities, as well as holiday flights.

Spring sunshine in the Central Gardens, Bournemouth. The River Bourne ('small river') runs through the Gardens before being piped under the Pier Approach and out to sea. Bourne Chine, as it was then known, was unenclosed common land and virtually deserted when in 1805 the Liberty of Westover was enclosed and sold. 205 acres, including the Gardens and much of the town centre, was bought by Sir George Tapps (1753-1835) for £1,050, and the first building was an inn named after him, The Tapps Arms. Six years later Lewis Tregonwell built Exeter House, Bournemouth's first house, followed by a handful of others – 'which he lets to persons who go for sea bathing'. In 1835 Sir George Tapps-Gervis (1795-1842) succeeded his father as Lord of the Manor and began building the 'marine villas' that formed the nucleus of the new town. By 1841 Bournemouth was being described as 'not only a watering-place, but . . . a winter residence for the most delicate constitutions requiring a warm and sheltered locality. . .'

Christchurch Priory from near the junction of the rivers Stour and Avon. The town's Saxon name was *Twinham*, or 'the place between the waters'. Yet despite its position and access to a sheltered harbour Christchurch's growth has, until recently, been slow. When the Priory was dissolved in 1539 the town was described as 'set in a desolate place . . . and slenderly inhabited', and it remained small and largely dependant on fishing and the cloth trade until the development of Bournemouth.

Christchurch Priory, the chancel from the south transept. The Regency memorial at the top of the steps is by Flaxman to Viscountess Fitzharris (died 1815) and shows her cradling one child whilst watched by her two sons. Beyond can be seen the carved stone reredos of about 1350. Amongst the other memorials in the priory is the glorious tomb of Margaret, Countess of Salisbury, the last of the Plantagenets. Despite being described by Henry VIII as the 'saintliest woman in England' and appointed governess to his daughter Mary, she finally fell from favour, ending her days aged 70 in 1541 on the executioner's block in the Tower.

The pilot boat alongside a Truckline ferry outward bound for Cherbourg from Poole, with Sandbanks and Poole Harbour in the background. The chain-ferry crossing the Harbour mouth is the only link between the built-up towns of Poole and Bournemouth and the still unspoilt Isle of Purbeck. Until early this century, Sandbanks was wild sand dunes, with only a handful of wooden shacks and the Coastguard Station – which until 1930 was housed in a beached Crimean gunboat.

The traditional heart of Poole, the Quay, showing the Harbour Office, Maritime Museum, and Customs House, with the church of St James in the background. The Harbour Office, which includes both the Fisheries Office and H.M.Coastguard was built in 1822, whilst the Maritime Museum is housed in what was the Town Cellars.

The Customs House, Poole Quay, rebuilt in 1813 after a fire and virtually identical to its late 18th century predecessor.

The Guildhall and Market Street, Poole. The Guildhall is now a museum, but the ground floor was once open and used as a meat market. This part of Poole is now a conservation area, and, hopefully, will avoid the fate of much of the old town, where in twenty years from 1950 over half the pre-1850s buildings were demolished.

The church of St James, Poole, rebuilt on a grander scale on the site of the old church in 1820, when the town's heyday as a port trading with Newfoundland was drawing to a close. A link with the trade is maintained by the pine pillars supporting the plaster vault, and which are thought to have been felled in Newfoundland as masts. The reasons for replacing the old church remain unclear, but must have given added impetus by the discovery of several open coffins beneath the floor of the pews from which 'an offensive smell arose'.

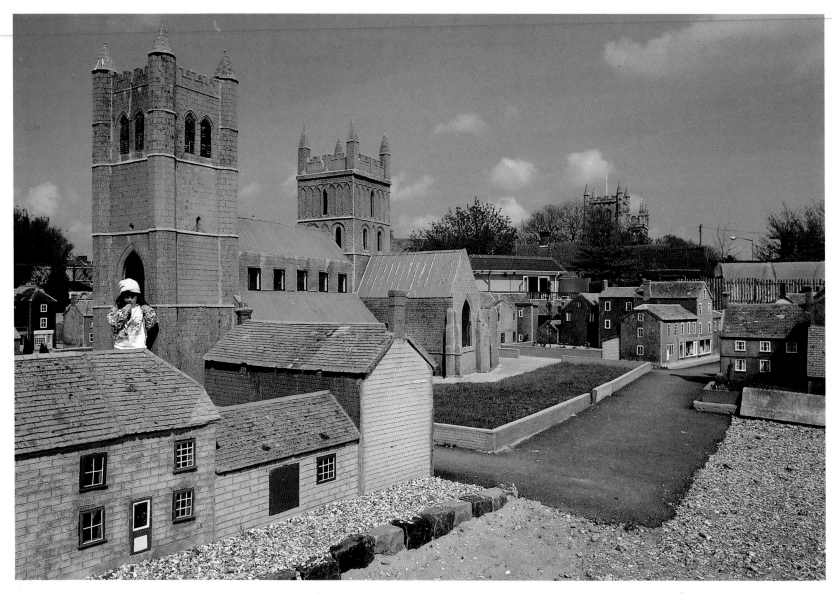

*Above* Wimborne Minster Model Town, King Street, with the real Minster just visible through the trees. The Model Town was originally built in 1951 on a garden allottment near the Cornmarket. The buildings were cast in concrete panels to a one tenth scale, providing a superb replica of what Wimborne actually looked like in the early 1950s, right down to the shop fronts. In 1983 the site behind the Cornmarket was sold, and the models had to be catalogued, removed, and stored. Sir Michael Hanham offered a new site on a pepper-corn rent, and in 1989 the Model Town was triumphantly resurrected.

*Opposite left* Morris dancers at Wimborne's annual Folk Festival dancing in the High Street.

*Opposite above right* The Quarter Jack on the north side of the bell tower, Wimborne Minster. The Jack, who strikes the quarter hours on his two bells, is first mentioned in 1612 when a Blandford carpenter was paid ten shillings (50p) for 'carving the Jack'. When first installed he was dressed as a monk, but was repainted in the uniform of a Grenadier as a sign of loyalty at the time of the Napoleonic Wars. The Minster is rich in unusual clocks. To the south is a rare three-sided sundial, whilst the dial of the 14th century astronomical clock in the Baptistry shows the sun and moon circling the central earth.

*Opposite lower right* The minster church of St Cuthberga, Wimborne Minster. The dedication is to a sister of Ine, King of Wessex, abbess of the Saxon monastery, which was founded in about 705 for both men and women. After the destruction of the abbey by the Vikings in the early 11th century, it was refounded by Edward the Confessor as a college of secular canons. None of the Saxon building survives, and the minster is largely Norman, although alterations continued throughout the Middle Ages. The saddest loss is the central spire, which is supposed to have rivalled Salisbury Cathedral's, and which fell in 1600.

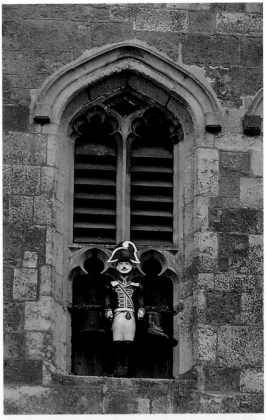

The Beech Avenue near Kingston Lacy on either side of the Wimborne/Blandford road. The Avenue stretches for 2 ½ miles and was planted by William Bankes in 1835. The great storms of 1987 and 1990 caused havoc the length of the Avenue, and duplicate lines have recently been planted by the National Trust.

A cottage on the edge of Pamphill Green. Despite being so close to Wimborne, Pamphill is delightfully rural, with a fine oak avenue planted in 1846 leading from the end of the Green to St Stephen's church, a cricket pitch, the manor house built by a 17th steward to the Bankes family, and a whole range of brick and timber-framed thatched cottages.

Kingston Lacy, the south front. The Kingston Lacy and Corfe Castle estates were given to the National Trust in 1981 by the late Ralph Bankes, forming one of the brightest jewels in the Trust's crown. Kingston Lacy, like Corfe Castle, was originally acquired in the 1630s by Sir John Bankes (1589-1644), Chief Justice to Charles I. The medieval manor house had long been in ruins and in the 1660s Roger Pratt designed an elegant brick replacement nearby for Sir Ralph Bankes (1631-1677). Between 1835-1841 the whole house was refaced in Chilmark stone by William Bankes (1786-1855) and his architect Charles Barry, transforming Kingston Lacy into the house that survives today. A strain of eccentricity has surfaced in many of the Bankes's, but never more remarkably than in William Bankes, a close friend of Lord Byron, who aptly nicknamed him 'the father of mischief'. William spent much of his life abroad, at first voluntarily in Spain, Egypt and Venice, then in exile in Venice after jumping bail rather than face trial for homosexuality. He is supposed to have landed illegally at Studland to visit the house, which he continued to fill with fine paintings and furniture. His father thought the arrival of the Egyptian obelisk, now on the south lawn, a symptom of a 'disorder in the Bankes family, which sometimes passes over one generation, like madness or gout, . . . and breaks out again in the next.'

*Left* Children from Sturminster Marshall First School dancing round the maypole on Sturminster Marshall Green. The water-rat on top of the pole is the village emblem.

*Lower left* White Mill on the River Stour near White Mill Bridge, Sturminster Marshall. The disused old corn mill is mid 18th century and the keystone of the archway over the mill-race is dated 1776. The Domesday Book records 280 Dorset mills, a figure which had halved by 1800 and is now reduced to only a handful.

*Below* White Mill Bridge, Sturminster Marshall. Cutwaters to break the flow divide the eight arches of the 16th century stone bridge. On top there are refuges for pedestrians. The bell from the ruined church at Knowlton supposedly lies in the deep water nearby following its theft by a party from Sturminster Marshall who intended taking it to France to sell. Villagers from Knowlton gave chase, forcing the robbers to drop the bell from the bridge, where it still remains. Hence the old doggerel:

> *Knowlton Bell is a-stole*
> *And thrown into Whitemill Hole.*
> *All the devils in hell*
> *Could never pull up Knowlton bell.*

Once a year, on the anniversary of the theft, a ghostly underwater tolling is supposedly audible to anyone standing on the bridge.

# CRANBORNE CHASE

# CRANBORNE CHASE

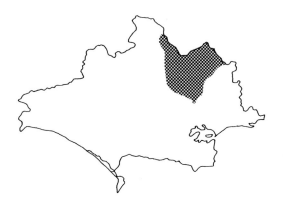

Early maps define the outer bounds of Cranborne Chase as Shaftesbury, Salisbury, Ringwood, Wimborne and Blandford. This immense area, of perhaps 250,000 acres, was gradually enclosed; but the wooded combes characteristic of the Chase still serve as reminders of the woodland that once covered much of what is now open downland rising to more than 900 feet.

From the Norman Conquest onwards strict laws governed the right to hunt the Chase deer. William the Conqueror gave the Chase to his queen, and it remained in royal hands until acquired by Robert Cecil, 1st Earl of Salisbury, from his patron James I. The medieval hunting lodge at Cranborne was enlarged so as to entertain the king, and Cranborne itself became the administrative capital of the Chase. In 1714 ownership of the Chase was inherited by George Pitt, and its later history is dominated by the Pitt-Rivers family.

The combination of remoteness and large numbers of deer turned the 18th century Chase into a 'nursery for ... all kinds of vice, profligacy and immorality.' Smugglers hid contraband brought inland from the coast. Isolated cottages housed 'nests of deer stealers, bred to it by their parents'. No one was immune to temptation. Squire Harbin of Eastbury Park used apple pulp left over from cider-making to lure deer into his park. In the churchyard at Sixpenny Handley is a tomb whose lid could be removed so as to hide the result of an illicit night's stalking. Pitched battles between poacher and keeper were commonplace. To defend themselves, the keepers carried staves, and wore padded canvas jackets and beehive hats made from straw bound with bramble stalks.

By the early 19th century the pressure for change was immense. The Pitt-Rivers' rights of 'vert and venison' meant that no one could clear and enclose land without risking falling foul of the law. In 1829 the Chase was disinfranchised and the reign of the fallow deer came to an end. Today, only a hundred or so remain, though the smaller roe are now probably more numerous than at any time in the past.

The Chase villages are few, and most are either spread along its western slopes or in the Allen and Tarrant valleys – where there are eight in ten miles. The most northerly, Tarrant Gunville, was the site of Eastbury Park, briefly Dorset's largest house; whilst only a barn survives of the once rich nunnery in the most southerly, Tarrant Crawford.

The towns which most naturally edge the Chase are Blandford and Shaftesbury. In 1731 Blandford was destroyed by fire, but from its ashes rose one of the most perfect Georgian towns in England. Shaftesbury is a true hilltop town, but there are few traces of its past. For it is here that King Alfred founded a nunnery that grew into the richest in England, and to which pilgrims flocked to see the bones of Edward the Martyr following his murder at Corfe Castle in 978.

*Previous page* The two storey brick gazebo on the east side of the Wimborne/Cranborne road (B3078) near Wimborne St Giles. The gazebo is thought to have been built by Anthony Ashley Cooper (1671-1713), 3rd Earl of Shaftesbury, who lived nearby at St Giles House, as a place in which to contemplate. The 'Philosopher Earl' is now little more than a historical footnote, but his most popular book, *Letters Concerning Enthusiasm*, ran to 11 editions, and in it he defined his main purpose as 'to learn what is just in society, and beautiful in Nature and the order of the world' – about as broad-based a philosophy as is possible. He died aged only forty-one, '. . . with perfect cheerfulness and the same sweetness of temper he always enjoyed in the most perfect health.'

The Iron Age hillfort of Badbury Rings, and now part of the National Trust's Kingston Lacy Estate. Despite the absence of any supporting evidence, Badbury Rings is still romantically linked with the legendary King Arthur's victory over the invading Saxons in about 500 AD – partly perhaps because ravens, traditionally associated with Arthur, continued to breed there until the 19th century.

The pump at Edmonsham dated 1884. Edmonsham lies on the eastern edge of the Chase where the chalk turns to clay, hence the fine oaks that grow locally – and the now defunct pottery industry, which had Verwood at its centre, and by 1750 numbered 15 working kilns.

Horses and their jockeys rounding the final bend at the Portman Hunt Point-to-Point at Badbury Rings. A number of point-to-point meetings are annually held near the huge Iron Age hillfort, and there are fine views out over the course.

Blandford Forum Market Place. The buildings surrounding the Market Place, like much of the town, owe their existence to a fire in 1713 and a second even more disastrous fire in 1731 in which all but a handful of houses were destroyed. The 1731 fire started in a tallow-chandler's shop, was fanned by a brisk wind, and spread quickly after engulfing a grocery containing a stock of gunpowder. The rebuilding was placed in the hands of two brothers, John and William Bastard, architect-builders based in the town, and they designed both the Town Hall and church of St Peter and St Paul. Just visible on the right is the roof of the Fire Monument, dated 1760, which records gratitude to 'DIVINE MERCY, that has raised this Town, like the Phoenix from it's Ashes, to it's present beautiful and flourishing State.'

The Greyhound, Blandford Forum Market Place. The original Greyhound was owned by the Bastard brothers at the time of the fire, and has the only post-fire facade to be rendered in stucco. Despite no longer being an inn, the carvings of bunches of grapes over the windows are reminders of its original purpose.

The ford through the River Tarrant at Tarrant Monkton. The little heath-stone footbridge is probably 17th century.

The 12th century church of St Mary, Tarrant Crawford. The great Cistercian nunnery founded by Richard Poore, Bishop of Salisbury, stood nearby. A coffin lid north of the altar is reputed to have come from the bishop's burial-place in the nunnery chapel, as is another that may have been part of the tomb of Queen Joan of Scotland, sister of Henry III. There are some lovely wall paintings inside the church telling the story of St Margaret of Antioch.

The Great Dorset Steam Fair, held at Southdown, Tarrant Hinton, every August, and now Dorset's most celebrated annual event, as well as the largest Steam Fair in Britain. The 150 engines it attracts consume 100 tons of coal and 250,000 gallons of water a day. Nearly 200,000 visitors attend the Steam Fair, which has raised more than £100,000 for charity since it started in 1969. Yet its beginnings were humble, and date back to the day Michael Oliver, John Pocock, Ted Hine, Charles Romanes and Ingram Spencer decided to build a rick at Stourpaine Bushes and thrash five acres of wheat by steam for the fun of it. So many people pulled up in their cars to watch that they booked some small advertisements and thrashed a further five acres a fortnight later. 28,000 people turned up and the Great Dorset Steam Fair had been born.

*Opposite above*  Ashmore Down to Fontmell Down. This is the classic Cranborne Chase landscape, a mixture of rolling open down with woodland cloaking the valley bottom.

*Opposite below*  The view west from near Sixpenny Handley over Wyke Down. The line of trees follows the route of Ackling Dyke, the main Roman road through Dorset which ran from London to Exeter via Old Sarum (near Salisbury), Badbury Rings and Dorchester. The road dates back to just after the Roman Conquest and was initially built to link the 2nd Legion at its base in Exeter with the capital. The road surface comprised fine gravel over larger foundation stones built up to form a ten feet wide causeway (the agger), with drainage ditches on either side. The section of Ackling Dyke between the eastern county boundary and Badbury Rings makes a superb walk along one of the finest stretches of undamaged Roman road in Britain.

*Above*  Ashmore pond. At 700 feet, the isolated hilltop village is the highest on Cranborne Chase. The village owes its name to the pond, from the Saxon *aesc* and *mere*, or the 'pool where ash trees grow'. The pond is nearly 16 feet deep on the rectory side, and it may well have Roman origins. Although only fed by rainwater, it rarely dries out. Traditionally, cakes were baked and eaten round its margin when it did, and local farmers hauled out the hundreds of cart-loads of silt that had accumulated on the bottom to manure their fields.

*Right*  R. A. Hudson, Ashmore's 'Grocer & General Stores', and the perfect example of a now endangered species – the village shop.

Cranborne Manor. The house dates back to about 1208 when it was used as a hunting lodge by King John. As one of the oldest surviving domestic buildings in England it is of immense architectural importance. Parts of the medieval house still exist, including the stair turret west of the porch, the battlements, a lancet chapel window, and a double window from which archers could cover the northern side of the house when under attack. Late in the reign of Elizabeth I, the house was acquired by her chief minister, Robert Cecil (1563-1612), 1st Earl of Salisbury, and the Manor that endures today is largely his creation. Robert Cecil served James I as loyally as he had Elizabeth, and the king nicknamed him 'My little beagle', partly because of his size (he was a hunchback and short), but also because of his ability to sniff out conspirators. The Manor he created at Cranborne is a delight, a fantasy of charm and exuberance. Above the Jacobean south loggia with its frieze and shell-headed niches there are a dozen roundels once filled with carvings of the signs of the Zodiac, of which two survive. The Manor was plundered during the Civil War and later divided into two farms. In 1863 the 2nd Marquess of Salisbury began repairing it, and his descendants still live in it today.

Visitors enjoying what surely ranks amongst the most exquisite gardens in England, those at Cranborne Manor. The main lines of the original 17th century garden laid out by John Tradescant still survive, but the succession of walks, enclosures and wild gardens that flourish today are largely the work of the 5th and 6th Marchionesses of Salisbury and the present Viscountess Cranborne.

Crichel House, Moor Crichel. The central part of the house was built by Sir William Napier in the middle of the 18th century to replace an earlier house that had been destroyed by fire. In 1765 it was inherited by Humphrey Sturt, of Horton, who after adding to his fortune by marrying an hieress proceeded to more than double the size of his house. At the same time he moved the entire village to New Town in Witchampton and created the landscaped park that surrounds the house.

The church of St Giles, Wimborne St Giles, and the adjoining almshouses. The almshouses were built in 1624, with five single rooms either side of the central entrance, by Sir Anthony Ashley (1551-1628), who is also credited with introducing cabbages into England and whose painted tomb is in the church next door. The church is largely the work of the Bastard brothers of Blandford in 1732 and Ninian Comper, who rebuilt it for the Shaftesburys following a fire in 1908. You will either like or loathe it, depending on your taste. There is a gallery, a profusion of monuments to the Earls of Shaftesbury and the Ashley-Cooper family, and an inscription near the altar in memory of a robin who continued nesting in the church whilst it was being rebuilt.

Horton Tower. The six storey folly had a fireplace halfway up and was built by Humphrey Sturt in the mid 18th century. Taylor's 1765 map of Dorset describes it as an 'Observatory', but according to one local legend it was built by Sturt as a viewing platform from which to watch the local hunt when too old to ride to hounds.

The derelict 12th century church at Knowlton, which stands inside the bank and ditches of a circular Neolithic henge monument. The old village of Knowlton stretched along the River Allen and may well have been abandoned after the Black Death. The church survived an attempt to demolish it in 1659, but finally succumbed when the roof collapsed in the late 18th century. The surrounding earthworks have never been excavated, but the whole area is obviously of considerable ceremonial or religious importance. The Bronze Age barrow known as the Great Barrow near the road is the largest in Dorset, and there are at least 40 others close to Knowlton Circles.

*Below* The surviving fragment of Eastbury Park, Tarrant Gunville, built by Vanbrugh for Bubb Dodington (1691-1792), 1st Lord Melcombe, and briefly the largest house in Dorset. Dodington was a Weymouth apothecary's son who by un-scrupulous political intriguing won wealth, power and a title. Eastbury was as flamboyant as its owner, and when complete extended to a massive 570 feet long central front incorporating five courtyards, as well as two groups of stables and outbuildings – of which the house that survives today is one. Despite having a succession of mistresses, Dodington never married, and left his creation to a nephew, Earl Temple, who lacked the money to keep it up. After vainly offering £200 a year to anyone who would take it off his hands, the earl was forced to have two thirds of it blown up in 1788. Photographs taken seventy years ago show the same pair of Scots pines above the gateway, without any apparent difference in their size.

*Right* Chettle House, Chettle, built in 1710 by Thomas Archer for the redoubtable George Chafin, MP and Ranger of Cranborne Chase. The Chafins were one of a group of families who did much in the early 18th century to bring fresh ideas backed by ample funds to Cranborne Chase. Hunting was their common obsession, and George Chafin's guardianship of the rights and privileges of the Chase led to collisions with his neighbour at Eastbury, Bubb Dodington, which on one occasion led Dodington to challenge him to a duel. A later owner of Chettle House was William Chafin (1733-1818), author of the best account of the battles that took place between keepers and deer-poachers, *Anecdotes and History of Cranborne Chase*, and a 'man mad upon sport.' William was even more rumbustious than his grandfather, and accidentally shot a woman on his first outing with a gun. As a punishment, he was locked in a garret for a month on bread and water – some of which he used to trap sparrows in an attempt to supplement his diet.

*Above* Shaftesbury High Street, with a storm building up over the windswept hilltop town. No other Dorset town has so fascinating yet elusive a history, which one early and imaginative writer claimed had been founded by King Lear's grandfather. In reality, Shaftesbury owes its creation to the fortress built by King Alfred and the nunnery he founded for one of his daughters. By the late Middle Ages it was Dorset's wealthiest town, and a place of veneration to the pilgrims who flocked to it to see the bones of Edward the Martyr. The Dissolution of the Monasteries in the 1530s swept away its churches, chapels, shrines and nunnery. Daniel Defoe found it a 'sorry' town when he visited in the early 18th century. Today it is an important market town, and the lovely Greensand houses in the centre are still largely residential.

*Left* Gold Hill, Shaftesbury. The wall on the right marked the edge of the Abbey precincts. Gold Hill is one of Dorset's most familiar – and photogenic – landmarks, and was originally one of the medieval roads into Shaftesbury. The name probably comes from coin-minters' workshops, and we know that a goldsmith from Bristol owned a tenement on the Hill during the 14th century.

*Below* Pump Court, St James, near the foot of Shaftesbury's Gold Hill. The pump is a reminder of the water shortage that once constantly troubled those living in the hilltop town. Water had to be carted in, from springs at Cann, a conduit at the foot of Castle Hill, or wells near Motcombe. Once a year the townsfolk went in procession to Enmore Green carrying a staff, or 'bezant', decorated with feathers, rings and pieces of gold. After dancing round the Green, they presented Motcombe with an annual payment of a raw calf's head, a pair of gloves, a gallon of beer and two penny loaves in return for the right to draw water. The procession was led by the 'Lord' and 'Lady', traditionally the town's most recently wed couple, in fine clothes decorated with ribbons and paid for by the Corporation.

Looking south-west out over St James and the Blackmore Vale from Park Walk, Shaftesbury. St James is mentioned as a parish in 1138, suggesting the early growth of a suburb at the foot of Gold Hill. A local rhyme once claimed that Shaftesbury was famous for:

*More strong beer than water*
*The churchyard higher than the church*
*More rogues than honest men.*

Lack of water was always a problem. St James churchyard is higher than the church, whilst the best comment on the townsfolks' reputation comes from a letter written in 1922 to John Udal, author of *Dorsetshire Folklore*, 'let us hope as regards the third that Shaftesbury has improved!'

# THE BLACKMORE VALE

# THE BLACKMORE VALE

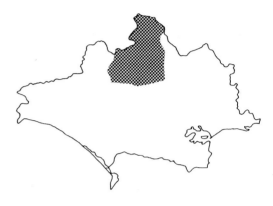

Look north from Bulbarrow on the edge of the chalk escarpment and the ground falls steeply, then levels into a patchwork of small irregular fields and high hedges that stretches away to the Somerset border. This is the Blackmore Vale, Hardy's 'Vale of the Little Dairies'. The dairies may now be larger, but they are still as numerous – as anyone who has confronted a milk lorry amongst the lanes will know.

Virtually all of the Vale has its feet in clay, and the claylands continue either side of the line of villages – from Todber in the east to Hazelbury Bryan in the west – that straddle the narrow limestone ridge in its centre. It is rich pastureland, drained by the Stour, Lydden and Divelish rivers, as well as the many brooks that twist amongst the meadows. William Barnes, the Dorset poet, who was born in 1801 just west of Sturminster Newton at Bagber, comes closer than anyone to evoking its character:

*Previous page* The typically agricultural face of the Blackmore Vale, Tom Coffin of Holwell.

*Left* Hammoon Manor, with its lovely late Tudor porch and thatched roof. The tiny hamlet lies amidst the water meadows on the Stour, and owes part of its name to the Saxon *hamm*, 'the enclosure or river meadow', and the rest to the Mohun family, whose manor it once was and who held it at the time of Domesday.

*Right* Purse Caundle Manor. According to tradition, an earlier house on the site was where sick or injured hounds were sent to recover when the 'king coursed wild beasts in Blackmore'. Their ghosts were later to be heard barking at midnight in the grounds. The earliest parts of the present house – including the Great Hall and Great Chamber, whose oriel window juts out over the lane – were built in about 1460 by the Long family. A south wing was added later, whose second storey was originally entered by a stone staircase. Half way up was a well inhabited by a fairy, and the staircase was demolished in the 19th century because the then owners disliked meeting the apparition as they went to bed.

*Below* The oldest pillar box still in use in Britain, at Barnes Cross, near Holwell. The octagonal box was made by John M. Butt & Co of Gloucester between 1853 and 1856, and is cast with Queen Victoria's cipher. The tiny letter slot is vertical.

> *Ov all the meads wi' shoals an' pools,*
> *Where streams did sheake the limber zedge.*
> *An' milken vo'k did teake their stools,*
> *In evenen sun-light under hedge:*
> *Ov' all the weirs the brook did vill,*
> *Or all the hatches where a sheet*
> *O' foam did leap below woone's veet,*
> *The pleace vor me wer Leeburn Mill.*

Much of the Vale, and the land round Gillingham, was once well-wooded. The present tapestry of field, farm and hedgerow oak owes its birth to the enclosure of the forest and waste during the Middle Ages. Only absent are the once common elms, and the wolf, two of which were killed as late as 1390. Both Blackmore and Gillingham were royal hunting forests, and the moated hunting lodge at Motcombe was substantial enough to merit the name King's Court Palace. Gillingham Forest was disafforested in 1624, and many of the large isolated farms in the area grew up as the land was cleared and enclosed. Blackmore's enclosure was more gradual, and although Barnes mourned the loss of the waste – 'Where we did use to run among / The vuzzen an' the broom', it created the wide verges typical of the Vale, and on which squatters later built cottages.

The Vale's capital is Sturminster Newton, locally shortened to 'Stur', and only Shillingstone, Marnhull and Stalbridge remotely approach it for size. But the Vale is best when most rural. Herons and kingfishers are common. Wild flowers flourish along the hedge-bottoms and in the water-meadows. It is a place of down-to-earth working farms, and it is they that have shaped its character.

*Above* Morning sunshine on Sturminster Newton Mill and its weir. The Domesday Survey of 1086 lists four mills on the River Stour at Sturminster Newton, three of them belonging to Glastonbury Abbey, of which this was probably one. The present working mill dates to the 17th century and contains two hammer mills, each with a dozen hammers. The water wheel was replaced in 1907 by a water turbine made locally in Ringwood by Joseph Armfield. It may be less attractive than a wheel, but is now of considerable interest as an example of fine engineering. In 1775 the weir pool was emptied and a bonfire lit on its base, 'accompanied by firing of cannon and an excellent band of music.'

*Left* Melbury Abbas Mill. The working watermill is open throughout the year, and has an attractive mill-pond with lots of ducks. The iron water wheel was installed in the late 19th century to work a circular saw.

*Right* The slopes of Hambledon Hill, showing part of the ditch and ramparts of the Iron Age hillfort. The Hill is where the Dorset Clubmen were routed by Cromwell in 1645 during the Civil War. Armed only with clubs, about 2,000 farmers and yeoman had banded together to protest at the plundering caused by the constant toing and froing of armies across Dorset. Cromwell finally lost his patience, calling them 'poor silly creatures'. In August he attacked them from the rear with 1,000 men. A dozen were killed, and some 300 taken prisoner and locked in Iwerne Courtney church, where Cromwell lectured them before allowing their release.

The southern side of the Iron Age ramparts on Hod Hill. The hollows and bumps on the right are quarry pits excavated to heighten the defenses. Archaeologists have unearthed large numbers of ballista bolts, the iron arrow-heads fired by the Romans, from the area round one of the largest Iron Age huts, suggesting a fierce battle when they attacked the hillfort. Following its capture, a legionary detachment of both foot-soldiers and cavalry built a Roman camp in one corner of the fort. The 54 acre site is now owned by the National Trust.

Cattle grazing the lush pasture in the Stour valley between Trill Bridge and Fifehead Magdalen.

Looking north towards Sturminster Newton from near Okeford Fitzpaine.

The lane leading down to Woolland and the Blackmore Vale from Bulbarrow Hill.

The Stour valley and Stour Provost. The little limestone village was originally called Stour *de Pratellis* or *de Preus*, after the abbey of St Leger at Preaux in France, who owned the manor in the 12th and 13th centuries. Edward IV (1461-1483) gave it to the Provost of King's College, Cambridge, who in turn sold it in 1925. Much of the land was then bought by Dorset County Council and let in 50 acre small holdings. Traditionally, there were endless disputes between the College and villagers over timber rights, and in 1812 the effigy of the College forester was hung in a tree and shot at by a crowd well-plied with cider.

*Left* Fiddleford Manor. The restored manor house is open to the public and is one of the earliest buildings in Dorset. In about 1355 the manor passed through marriage to William Latimer, sheriff of Somerset and Dorset in 1374 and 1380, and the late 14th century Great Hall and Solar were built for him. Both rooms have 600-year-old timber roofs with collar-beam trusses and timber-work of great complexity and beauty. Originally the smoke from the central fire seeped out through a louvre in the roof. The Manor was remodelled in both the 16th and 17th centuries, and despite being unfurnished is still fascinating as it gives the best feel in the county of what it must have been like to live in a medieval house.

*Below left* Duncliffe Hill from Langham. The Hill is visible from all over north-east Dorset and in clear weather there are panoramic views from its 710 feet (210 metres) summit. An old weather rhyme ran:

> *If Duncliff wood be fair and clear*
> *You Stour boys need have no fear*
> *But if Duncliff wood doth wear it's cap*
> *You Marnhull folk look out for that.*

*Left* The 14th century church of St Mary Magdalen, Fifehead Magdalen, on the limestone ridge overlooking the Stour. The village, like neighbouring Fifehead Neville, is named after its Domesday assessment of five hides (a hide was the amount of land that could be tilled by one plough in a year – normally 100 acres). The north chapel was built in 1730 to house a monument to the Newman family, one of whom, Richard, was a leader of the Dorset Clubmen.

*Above* Looking west out over the Blackmore Vale from Kington Magna churchyard. Recent archaeological work has established that there was once a medieval settlement in the field south-west of the church. At some point, probably early in the 15th century, the settlement was abandoned and in part replaced by a fishpond, much of which survives. A volume of sermons preached by a 17th century vicar of Kington Magna, Aldrich Swan, is now in the Chained Library in Wimborne Minster.

In one, speaking of women, he said, '. . . 'tis observed of that sex, that either natural weakness and violence of passion make them exceedingly sinful; or else their natural timidity and modesty render them as highly virtuous.'

# FISHING

he whole of Dorset's southern border is coastal, and the sea has yielded a rich harvest to those who live alongside it.

*If Poole was a fish pool, and the men of Poole fish*
*There's be a pool for the Devil and fish for his dish.*

So ran an old rhyme, commenting more on Poole's reputation for piracy than its ability to land a catch. But of all Dorset's ports, Poole has most successfully exploited the sea. From early in the 17th century its fishing fleet annually went to Newfoundland, each boat carrying as much sail as it dared in order to be first to the best fishing grounds. They returned with furs, train oil and salted fish, much of which was landed in the Mediterranean in exchange for wine. Some Poole merchants made fortunes, for in its heyday 200 ships and 1,500 men were dependant on the Newfoundland trade. Today, only a handful of local boats land their catches at the quay, and the oyster beds for which the Harbour was once famous are no longer farmed.

The other great annual event in the coastal calendar was the first sighting of the mackerel shoals, usually in April off Chesil. Look-outs were posted on the hills above Abbotsbury, where on Old May Day the children tossed garlands of flowers overboard from the boats crewed by their family into the sea as an offering. Once a shoal had been spotted, all other work was abandoned, and the crews put to sea in sturdy rowing boats called lerrets, built double-ended so that they could be launched stern first through the

Weighing and loading spider crabs on Weymouth Quay. Most are exported, either to France or Spain.

A fishing boat passing the Customs House on Poole Quay on its way out to sea.

Salmon fishermen hauling in their nets on the edge of the Run, near the entrance to Christchurch Harbour between Mudeford and Hengistbury Head. Six licenses are currently granted to net salmon between February 1st and July 1st, continuing a tradition described in the late 19th century as the 'most ancient and primitive fishery.' The netting is usually done by a team of three, one holding the net on the bank, whilst the others row furiously across the channel as the ebb tide spills through the entrance. The rewards are meagre, with 266 fish being taken in 1990. The only other place in Dorset where salmon are netted is in Poole Harbour at the mouth of the River Frome.

rollers. One end of the net was towed in a half circle, the other held taut on the beach. Immense numbers of fish were once landed, and in a good season the daily catches often totalled 250,000. Mackerel are still caught, but not in such quantity, although anglers fishing for cod and bass still line the Chesil in all weathers. The waters off Purbeck are well-known for their shellfish, and Weymouth still has a small fishing fleet, despite the disappearance of the red mullet for which the Bay was once renowned.

Dorset's rivers are a fisherman's delight, both for game and coarse fish. At Mudeford, at the mouth of Christchurch Harbour, salmon are netted in season from the beginning of the ebb until the tide turns. Salmon are also caught in the rivers, particularly the Frome, but the Piddle, Allen and all the chalk streams offer fine trout fishing. There is hardly a river without pike, and the record roach was caught on the Stour. But few fishermens' tales are likely to equal the 203 pound sturgeon caught on the Frome in 1911 and now stuffed and on display in the Dorset County Museum.

*Above* A lone fisherman hoping for an evening catch off the Chesil Beach.

*Above right* Casting a dry fly on the River Allen.

*Right* Inspecting nets at the Bridport-Gundry Mill, Bridport. Bridport-made nets are used by fishing fleets all over the world. The green net is a trawl, but Birdport-Gundry also make a whole range of other nets, including the arrester nets used by the Space Shuttle and those at the Wimbledon Tennis Championships.

*Below* A fishing boat at anchor in Lulworth Cove.

# SHERBORNE AND THE NORTHERN BORDERS

# SHERBORNE AND
# THE NORTHERN BORDERS

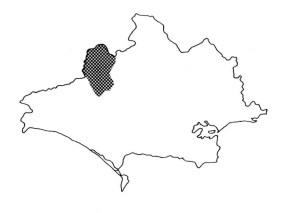

Both south of Sherborne to the edge of the chalk, and north to the Somerset border, lies an area of rich farmland whose low wooded hills hide some of Dorset's loveliest stone villages: Yetminster, Trent, Leigh and the Comptons.

In 705 a Benedectine monk named Aldhelm, a member of Wessex's ruling family, was consecrated first Bishop of Sherborne. His new diocese was immense, covering all of Dorset and Somerset, and probably both Devon and Cornwall. Few fragments of the Saxon cathedral begun by Saint Aldhelm survive, but the great abbey church now standing on the site is architecturally the most important building in Dorset, and famous for its gorgeous fan vaulting, monuments and stalls. Like the Abbey, much of Sherborne is built of stone, whilst on the edge of the town are the two castles that share its name. One was built by a Bishop of Salisbury as a fortified palace and is now a ruin, whilst the other will always be associated with its builder, the ill-fated Sir Walter Raleigh.

The lovely orange stone from Ham Hill and the limestone quarries round Sherborne give the area its character. A stone gatehouse guards the entrance to the Elizabethan manor house at Sandford Orcas. Stone cottages are scattered through Rhyme Intrinsica, whose odd name refers to it being inside the manor of Rhyme, as opposed to outside it (extrinsica). The stone church at Stockwood is Dorset's smallest, and the second smallest in England. Nearby is Bubb Down Hill, from whose summit the view extends out over the Jacobean manor house at its foot to where the aptly named River Wriggle winds along its valley.

*Previous page* The door in the west tower, the church of St Mary, Bradford Abbas – a name derived from the land beside a *broad ford* on the Ivel given to Sherborne Abbey by King Alfred. Two of the eleven niches in the 15th century tower still retain their original figures, and the Ham Hill stone church is amongst the most beautiful in north Dorset. Ironically, two members of the same family who took opposite sides in the Monmouth Rebellion lie buried beneath the chancel: Michael Harvey, who entertained Monmouth at Clifton Maybank in 1680; and William Harvey, who was killed by the rebels in a skirmish at Bridport whilst serving in the militia.

*Left* The Conduit, Sherborne. Originally situated in the Abbey cloisters, the Conduit was moved to the Parade in about 1560 to pipe water to the School and part of the town. In the 1840s it became a reading room, and by the end of the century had seen service as the town lock-up, a penny bank and a depot for stuffing pillows for those wounded in the Franco-Prussian War of 1871.

Sherborne and the Abbey from the slopes of Dancing Hill. Sherborne owes its existence to the Saxon cathedral built when St Aldhelm was consecrated first Bishop of the newly created see of Wessex in 705. Two Saxon kings were buried in the church, but the only surviving pre-Conquest portion is a doorway or archway in the west wall. In 998 a Benedictine monastery was established in its shadow, and from early in the 12th century the Abbey was gradually rebuilt. In 1075 the see was transferred to Old Sarum (Salisbury), perhaps because the cathedral had failed to encourage the growth of a town. In 1125 Sherborne was described as a 'small village lacking people'. A century later the great bishop of Salisbury, Richard Poore, established a new borough at Newland. By 1450 Sherborne was Dorset's most populated town, with a market, shambles, shops, and a number of fulling mills that had been built as the cloth trade flourished. It is no longer Dorset's largest town, but it is certainly the most attractive, with a whole range of lovely stone buildings. Although usually quiet, despite large numbers of schoolchildren, Sherborne comes to life for the October Pack Monday Fair, named either after the travelling packmen who toured country fairs, or the celebrations enjoyed by the masons when they 'packed up' after a season spent working on the Abbey. Traditionally it started at midnight, after which 'the riotous expenses and unlawful games' of those attending meant that few of the townsfolk enjoyed much sleep.

The glorious 15th century fan vaulting in the nave of Sherborne Abbey.

The Almshouse of St John, Sherborne. The almshouse was refounded in 1438 to support '12 poor, feeble, impotent men and four poor, feeble, impotent women', and is still in use today.

Upbury Farm, Yetminster, the oldest of the many locally quarried limestone farmhouses in the village, and originally an open hall house. The doorway and two blocked windows are 15th century, and Upbury was probably built by a canon of Salisbury Cathedral as a country retreat.

The landscape near Leigh in early February. Leigh, and neighbouring Chetnole, mark the western rim of a wide band of Oxford Clay that extends east to Lydlinch. The villages sit on the few patches of gravel, and tend to have small centres and numerous scattered farms. The clay meant ample water for dairy farming, with about 2 ½ acres of pasture providing the hay and grazing for each cow. Thus a 40 cow dairy required 100 acres, which is typical of the farms in the area.

The church of St Andrew, Trent, with the Priest's House of 1500 on one side of the churchyard. The copper weathercock on top of the spire is dated 1698. A painted notice in the porch asks that 'All persons are requested to take off, Pattens and Clog's before entering the church.'

Folke, the manor and church. The small isolated village lies half-way between Longburton and Alweston. The manor house was started in the early Tudor period, but was altered and extended in the 17th century, when the church was also rebuilt. There is an old tradition that the church foundations were laid in a nearby wood, but that what was built by day was moved to its present site during the night.

Sherborne Castle, built by Sir Walter Raleigh in the 1590s and the home of the Digby family since shortly before Raleigh's execution in 1618. The great Elizabethan poet, sailor and adventurer had been granted a lease on the Old Castle, which is now a ruin, by Elizabeth I. His secret marriage to Elizabeth Throgmorton led to his fall from favour and he was banished from Court. He soon abandoned his attempt to repair the Old Castle, building a new home on the site of an early Tudor hunting lodge, and both the main block and the corner turrets date back to Raleigh's original house. The interior is very much the creation of successive Digbys, and includes four fine drawing rooms as well as the lovely 18th century Strawberry Hill-Gothic Library.

Sandford Orcas Manor, built by Edward Knoyle in Ham Hill stone in the mid 16th century, and owned by the Medlycott family for the last 250 years. A garderobe, or privy, projects from the far wall of the gate house. Next door in the church there is a monument to William Knoyle (died 1607) with his two wives and eleven children, four of whom are shown dead in swaddling clothes.

Melbury Bubb and the valley of the River Wriggle
from Bubb Down, with the Jacobean manor house
and the church of St Mary.

# THE MARSHWOOD VALE
# AND WEST DORSET

# THE MARSHWOOD VALE
## AND WEST DORSET

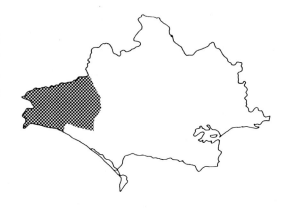

The Marshwood Vale and much of west Dorset are the county's best kept secret. The inland roads from the coast swiftly turn into narrow sunken lands linking scattered villages and hamlets. As its name implies, the Vale is marshy and well-wooded, and was described by John Hutchins, the great 18th century Dorset historian, as a 'deep inclosed country, formerly hardly passable by travellers but in dry summers'. The Vale farms are framed by the encircling hills, which at Lewesdon Hill and Pilsdon Pen, Dorset's highest points, reach over 900 feet. The coastal towns of Lyme Regis and Bridport turn their backs on the Vale, and its only town is Beaminster, whose description by William Barnes lyrically evokes the character of the surrounding countryside:

*Sweet Be'mi'ster, that bist a-bound*
*By green an' woody hills all round,*
*Wi' hedges reachen up between*
*A thousan' vields o'zummer green.*

*Previous page* Coney's Castle, a small Iron Age hillfort in the Marshwood Vale belonging to the National Trust. A modern lane cuts through the centre of the camp, but its western slopes are lovely for picnics, with fine views out over the Vale. Coney is an old word for a rabbit.

*Left* Beaminster from White Sheet Hill, showing the 'green an' woody hills all round' described by William Barnes. Beaminster is a small town with a long history, and is first mentioned in a 9th century Saxon charter, which in turn links it to an existing minster, perhaps founded by an abbess, Bebba. Of all Dorset's towns, Beaminster is the least changed, and though ravaged by fire in 1644 and 1781 the centre is small-scale and rich in 17th and 18th century stone houses and shops.

Typical of these summer-green fields is the land at Lower Kingcombe bought by the Dorset Trust for Nature Conservation in 1987 amidst much publicity, and now preserved as the last intact area of unspoilt lowland meadow in southern England. The very west of the county, where the River Axe forms the Devon boundary, is equally unspoilt, with rounded hills acting as a backdrop to Forde Abbey and its gardens. Fine gardens are plentiful throughout west Dorset. At Parnham they surround the lovely Tudor manor, whilst at Mapperton the Jacobean house overlooks the extraordinary formal gardens that fill the valley.

From early in the Middle Ages Bridport was famous for net and rope-making, hence those who ended their days on the gallows were said to have been 'stabbed by a Bridport dagger'. Hemp and flax were grown nearby, and the rope exported from a small port on the River Brit whose survival was dominated by the struggle to stop the river silting up.

Lyme Regis's prosperity was also at the mercy of the elements. Its famous artificial harbour, the Cobb, was originally built from massive boulders placed inside walls made from oak-trunks, and without it Lyme would have had neither harbour nor protection from south-westerly storms. The Regis dates back to the royal charter granted it by Edward I in 1284 which gave it freedom from customs and duties, but its heyday as a port trading in wool and wine was over by 1700. By the end of the 18th century the fashion for sea-bathing had made it into the resort town visited by Jane Austen, and brought it the first of the many holidaymakers who still flock there today. Between the two towns lies the high Greensand cliff of Golden Cap, and a string of tiny beaches formed where small rivers and streams enter the sea; West Bay, Eype Mouth, Seatown and Charmouth.

The 12th century font at Toller Fratrum. The Fratrum comes from 'brothers', who were the knights of St John of Jerusalem and owners of the manor in the Middle Ages. The tiny village consists of a few cottages, a Tudor farm with its thatched stable block and barn, and the small church of St Basil. The crudely carved figures on the font completely encircle it, and on one side there is a two-bodied monster with one head.

Parnham House, near Beaminster, showing the entrance porch with its fine early Tudor oriel window. The house was built by Sir Robert Strode in the 1550s, the most successful of a family of small farmers who owed their wealth to good husbandry, astute purchase and marriage to women with money – one of whom, Ann Strode, was beheaded during the Civil War in the Great Hall by a Parliamentarian soldier. In 1976 it was bought by the furniture designer John Makepeace, and is now the home of the John Makepeace Furniture Workshops. It has glorious gardens that stretch down to the River Brit. Nearby in the park is the burial place of William Rhodes Moorhouse, the first airman to be awarded the Victoria Cross.

The Cobb, Lyme Regis, showing its remarkable serpentine shape, with Golden Cap and the cliffs between Seatown and Eype's Mouth in the background. The Cobb is the setting of the arresting opening scene in which Sarah Woodruff and Charles Smithson first meet in John Fowles's novel *The French Lieutenant's Woman* (1969).

Marine Parade, or the Walk, Lyme Regis. The town is first mentioned in Saxon times in connection with salt rights, but owes its growth to the royal charter granted to it by Edward I in 1284. Its most prosperous period was from 1500 to 1700, when its merchants and sea captains traded with the Mediterranean, West Indies and Americas. Typical of the breed was Sir George Somers ('a lamb on land, . . . a lion at sea') who discovered the Bermudas, and was born in Lyme. The town withstood a Royalist siege during the Civil War, but paid for its independence in 1685 after the failure of the Monmouth Rebellion. The Duke landed at Lyme, and 23 rebels were later hung and quartered on the beach where he first stepped ashore. The town's later decline was halted in the 18th century when sea-bathing became fashionable. Two centuries later Lyme still relies on summer visitors for its survival.

Heavy seas breaking over the Cobb, Lyme Regis. The Cobb is first mentioned in the reign of Edward III (1327-1377), when it was described as a work of timber and stone damaged by storms. The stones were actually huge boulders, called cowstones, brought to the site by being floated between barrels and then stacked loose between oak piles. The Cobb was initially detached from the shore at high tide to let shingle through, which in turn formed protective banks or sea defences. For Lyme is totally exposed to south-westerly gales, and the Cobb is both harbour and breakwater. In 1377 it was destroyed in a storm, leading to the destruction of 80 houses and 50 boats. The presence of the Cobb allowed Lyme Regis to become a shipbuilding centre and important port, trading wool for wine. In 1756 the Cobb was finally joined to the land, and beginning in 1820 it was completely rebuilt in Portland stone.

Tess Cottage, Evershot, and the church of St Osmond.

*Above* The remote hamlet of North Poorton near Powerstock. The church of St Mary Magdelene was rebuilt in the 19th century by the Dorchester architect John Hicks, for whom Thomas Hardy was then working.

*Right* Looking out over Corscombe. Corscombe was where Thomas Hollis (1720-1774), the great democrat and Republican, spent the last years of his life. He died whilst out walking and, at his own wish, lies buried at an unknown spot in an unmarked grave in a field near the village. Hollis was a great benefactor to many universities, including Harvard, and named his fields after his beliefs – hence Republican, Revolution and others. He loathed London, but owned property in Lyme Regis, whose decline he reversed by persuading the Earl of Chatham to bring his sickly son to the town for the sea air: the son was William Pitt the Younger.

Broadwindsor, with the 15th century tower of the church of St John the Baptist. The Royalist poet and author of *A History of the Worthies of England*, Thomas Fuller (1608-1661), was rector from 1634-1642. The 'Worthy Doctor' was popular in the parish, and there is still a tradition that his congregations were so large he used to preach from the steps. In turn, the villagers welcomed him into their cottages, and he noted that their affections were 'much warmed in a good kitchen, and turneth much on the hinges of a buttery-door often open.' As well as being a noted wit, he was also wise: 'He that falls into sin is a man; that grieves at it, is a saint; that boasteth of it, is a devil.' In the village centre is a cottage recalling the night Charles II slept there in 1651 when a fugitive.

the Wallbridges, Arthur, died on Christmas Day 1985 and shortly afterwards the entire estate was bought by a London property speculator, who in turn promptly broke it up into lots and put it to auction. Local concern turned to national outcry as Lower Kingcombe's importance became known. The Dorset Trust for Nature Conservation launched a world-wide appeal, and with the £320,000 raised successfully bought 327 acres. It remains a unique survival, and is now run by the Trust as a nature reserve whose livestock graze the last untouched area of lowland meadow in southern England.

*Opposite above* Forde Abbey. The Cistercian abbey was founded in 1136 when a small group of monks were returning to Surrey after the failure of an abbey in Devon. Half-starved and bedraggled, they were taken pity on by Adelicia de Brionca, who gave them her manor of Thorncombe. They built their new monastery on land beside the Axe, where a ford crossed the river. Only the vaulted chapter house, now a chapel, from the original Abbey survives, and the south front is dominated by the porch tower and hall built by Abbot Chard shortly before the Abbey was dissolved and converted into a house. Successive owners have continued to add to it, and the fine Mortlake tapestries given to Francis Gwyn by Queen Anne hang in the magnificent 17th century saloon. In 1906 the house was left to Mrs Freeman Roper, whose descendants still own it. The gardens extend to about 40 acres, and are a delight, with fine trees, naturalized flowers, cascades, and ponds formed from the old monastic fishponds.

*Opposite below* The formal gardens, Mapperton House, near Beaminster. The gardens are in part the creation of Mrs Ethel Labouchere from 1926 onwards, and, more recently, Victor Montagu, who bought Mapperton after her death in 1955. A classical Orangery built in 1966 stands at the head of the valley, and looks down the length of the Italianate gardens laid out by Mrs Labouchere in memory of her husband. The formal gardens fall in descending levels down the valley, the ponds shown here giving way to a grassy walk edged with fine trees that gradually fades away into the Dorset countryside. The manor house, which looks down over the gardens, was begun by Robert and Mary Morgan in the mid 16th century, who afterwards had the following inscription placed in the hall:
> *What they spent, that they lent;*
> *What they gave, that they have;*
> *What they left, that they lost.*

*Above* The River Hook at Lower Kingcombe. In 1918 the then tenant of Lower Kingcombe Farm, John Wallbridge, bought the 446 acre farm from the Earl of Sandwich, when it was described as 'a famous dairy farm noted for its Dorset Blue Cheese and Butter.' The hedgerows, fields and hay meadows remained miraculously intact, unsprayed and untouched by artificial fertilisers. The last of

*Left* South Street, Bridport. The town grew up round the rope industry, which developed during the Middle Ages following King John's request that the townsfolk make 'night and day as many ropes for ships both large and small and as many cables as you can.' Hemp and flax were grown locally, and the ropes were originally laid in long rope walks extending from the backs of houses. Bridport was at its most prosperous in the 18th and 19th centuries, which is when many of the houses in South Street were built.

*Opposite below* The harbour at West Bay. Originally Bridport Harbour, its name was changed by the Great Western Railway in 1884 when the railway was extended, so as to distinguish it from the town and suggest a holiday resort rather than a small working port. The first harbour, or 'haven', was built in the 14th century, but its fortunes fluctuated – pirates, plague, storms and a lack of funds leading one writer to describe it as not deserving 'the name of port'. Bridport's growth as a rope and net-making centre led to the harbour's gradual improvement. The River Brit was diverted, piers and wharves were constructed, and the port was at its most prosperous in the early 19th century. Today, a few fishing boats and small sailing boats use the harbour, but because it is so exposed, and the piers guarding the entrance are only 60 feet apart, it is as difficult to leave as it is to enter in all but the calmest weather.

*Right* The outline of a fossilised ammonite on the beach east of Lyme Regis. Not only is the land round Lyme remarkably unstable, it is also rich in fossils, attracting both professional palaeontologists and amateur fossil-seekers content to forage for finds between tides. There are two fossil shops in the town, continuing a tradition begun by Lyme-born Mary Anning, who in 1828 found the rarest of all local vertebrate fossils, that of a pterosaur, or 'winged lizard'.

Golden Cap from Charmouth beach. At 625 feet (191 metres) Golden Gap is the highest point on the south coast, and owes its name and colour to the capping of Upper Greensand. Both the Cap and the surrounding land belong to the National Trust. The whole area offers lovely walks, with plenty of footpaths, seats, wild flowers, and fields farmed by traditional methods. On the western slopes are what remain of the little village of Stanton St Gabriel, which was bypassed by the road, and is now only a farmhouse, cottage and ruined late-medieval church. In clear weather, the views are unrivalled, with Hay Tor on Dartmoor 41 miles to the west, Lewesdon Hill to the north, and Portland and Chesil Beach to the east.

*Right* The Marshwood Vale from Pilsdon Pen, with the sea in the distance.

*Below* Racedown House, near Birdsmoorgate, with the slopes of Payne's Down rising above the tiny River Synderford. Racedown was built in 1758 by John Frederick Pinney, MP for Bridport, and grandson of Azariah Pinney, a supporter of Monmouth and sentenced to transportation to the West Indies in the wake of the 1685 Rebellion. Following the MPs death in 1762, Racedown was inherited by a nephew, John Pretor Pinney, a Bristol merchant and slave-owner, who regarded Racedown as 'a lee-port in a storm' and added a third storey. The house is best known for having been lived in by William and Dorothy Wordsworth from 1795 to 1797. It was here Wordsworth wrote *The Borderers* and many of the 'Lyrical Ballads'. They walked constantly, but were greeted with suspicion by the locals, for William carried a small pocket telescope with which he was suspected of bewitching cattle, 'whilst his habit of speaking poetry aloud as he walked was extremely puzzling to them.'

*Below right* The 13th century shrine of St Wite in Whitchurch Canonicorum church, known locally as 'the cathedral' of the Marshwood Vale. The stone chest contains the saint's skeleton, and the openings were for pilgrims to put their diseased limbs into in hope of a cure. Such shrines are rare, for most were destroyed during the Reformation.

The sun breaking through the clouds massed over the ramparts of the Iron Age hillfort on Eggardon Hill.

Bettiscombe and Conegar Hill. Bettiscombe is tiny, just the church, farmhouse and a scattering of cottages. The track in the foreground leads to Bettiscombe House, a lovely brick house built by the Pinney family in the beginning of the 18th century.

# THE SOUTHERN COAST

# THE SOUTHERN COAST

Stand on Portland Heights with your back to the rest of the 'Island' and Royal Manor and you look out over one of England's most remarkable sights, the eight mile length of Chesil Beach. The Beach is a massive shingle ridge that links Portland to the mainland and stretches west to Abbotsbury. The pebbles get smaller as you go west, allowing locals to always know where they are. Behind it lies the Fleet, a long brackish lagoon that near Abbotsbury provides nesting sites for the Swannery. Wrecks were once common along Chesil, leading to scenes of looting that only ended when five wreckers died from drunkenness following the loss of the *Royal Adelaide* in 1872. Occasionally the sea broke through, as at Fleet, where the village was swept away and only part of the church remains.

Tucked inland from the Chesil is the lovely Bride Valley, with Little Bredy at its head and Burton Bradstock where it reaches the sea. The whole valley is consistently beautiful, a mixture of down, woodland, and stone and thatch villages. Virtually all that survives of the abbey that gave Abbotsbury its name is the barn with its pond and the 14th century St Catherine's Chapel overlooking the village. For those who can face the climb the reward is a superb hilltop view across Lyme Bay and east toward Portland.

*Previous page* Early 19th century houses lining the south side of Weymouth Harbour.

*Left* Great Barn, Abbotsbury. Apart from the Great Barn, gatehouse, and St Catherine's Chapel, only fragments remain of the Benedictine Abbey, originally founded by Ore, King Canute's steward, in about 1026. The barn was built at the start of the 15th century and was 272 feet long, though half is now in ruins. Following its Dissolution in 1539 the abbey lands were acquired by Sir Giles Strangways, whose descendants still own them today.

Looking west towards St Catherine's Chapel and Abbotsbury, with the Swannery on the left in the lee of Chesil Beach. The 400-800 mute swans who breed at the Swannery continue a tradition begun by the monks in the 14th century, when swans were bred for eating. Once the cygnets have hatched, the Swannery is open so that visitors can walk amongst the nests and watch the swanherds feeding and checking the flock.

A clue to Portland's character lies in a 16th century description of its inhabitants: 'The people be good there in flyngging of stonys, and use it for defence of the isle'. The 'Island' is a solid block of limestone jutting out into the Channel, and its isolation until the 19th century made Portlanders mistrustful of outsiders, or 'Kimberlins'. One Portland custom was that women did not marry until pregnant, after which 'she tells her mother; the mother tells her father; her father tells his father; and he tells his son, that it is then the proper time to be married'.

The Island's quarrying industry dates back to medieval times, but the boom years followed Christopher Wren's decision to rebuild St Paul's Cathedral in Portland stone after the Great Fire of 1666. Since then millions of tons have been shipped from its quays, and a handful of the quarries are still being worked. The Breakwater was built in the 19th century to provide a safe naval anchorage, and much of the work on both the Breakwater and Verne fortifications was done by convict labour drawn from the prison.

Weymouth is, with Bournemouth, Dorset's most popular resort, but the fine sands and Esplanade are where the town refuse was once dumped. It was originally two separate ports, Melcombe Regis and Weymouth, whose decline was only halted when George III chose to spend his summer holidays in the town. The birth of 'Royal Weymouth' and the arrival of wealthy visitors eager to try 'sea-bathing' transformed it into the most fashionable resort in the country. But fashion is fickle, and Weymouth today is a mixture of working town, resort and port, with the finest sea-front in Dorset.

St Catherine's Chapel, Abbotsbury, overlooking
the Fleet and Chesil Beach, with Portland in the
distance. The Chapel was built by the Abbey in the
14th century and survived the Dissolution because
it made a good sea-mark. Once a year, spinsters
climbed up to the Chapel to pray for a husband:

> *A husband, St Catherine;*
> *A handsome one, St Catherine;*
> *A rich one, St Catherine;*
> *A nice one, St Catherine;*
> *And soon, St Catherine!*

Weymouth, the beach and Esplanade. A poem written by the clown Joe Grimaldi in the late 18th century extolling Weymouth's delights remains equally apt today:

> But the place of all places for me,
> Is Weymouth, so handsome and gay,
> Where you sniff the salt air of the sea,
> And drive your complaints all away.

To the left of the Jubilee Clock stands Gloucester Lodge, where George III stayed on his first visit in 1789, thus transforming Weymouth into the most fashionable resort in England.

Weymouth Harbour. Until the town became a resort, the Harbour area was its commercial heart, but more recently its fortunes have fluctuated. The great sailing ships bringing in grain and timber from the Baltic are a thing of the past, as are the sprit-sail barges that once shipped in coal and cement, but it still remains crowded with fishing and crabbing boats. The brick-built building on the left with the bow window looking out over the Quay is the 18th century Customs House. Regular auctions of contraband seized by Customs men were once held here – a sale in 1832 included 1501 gallons of brandy.

The old fishing village of Chiswell, and Chesil Beach, from Portland Heights, with the Royal Naval Air Station built on land reclaimed from the tidal Mere on the right. Until the building of the first bridge at Smallmouth in 1839, Portland was virtually isolated from the rest of Dorset, making Portlanders fiercely independent and wary of outsiders. 'They are,' wrote the Dorset historian John Hutchins, 'a stout hardy industrious race, and in general better informed than most labouring people; very healthy, but not long-lived, for though at 60 many of the men appear strong and robust, they soon drop off . . . which may be accounted for from too great a use of spirits.' In 1824 36 houses in Chiswell were destroyed and 26 people drowned when gigantic waves crashed over the Beach during the Great Gale. Despite the building of a sea wall in 1960, the village remained vulnerable to high tides and south-westerly storms, and was flooded twice in the 1970s – since when the sea defences have been strengthened.

450 years of Portland history. In the foreground is Portland Castle, built by Henry VIII in the 1540s to defend Weymouth Harbour against attack. The big building to its left is an accomodation block for HMS *Osprey* and the Naval Dockyard. Portland first became a Naval Base in 1871, following the completion of the Breakwater. The massive defences on the hill behind, the Verne, were built by convict labour in the mid-19th century to guard the Harbour, and the heart of the citadel is still in use as a prison. The white dome on the summit is a modern Radar link used by the Naval Base.

*Below* St George's Church, Reforne, Portland. The church was built between 1754 and 1766 to replace the Norman church of St Andrew above Church Ope Cove on the east side of the Island, which was threatened by cliff falls. St George's was designed by a Portlander, built from Portland stone by local masons, and remains one of the most superb pieces of Georgian architecture in Dorset – despite being redundant since 1917. The inside is as striking as the outside, with three galleries, box pews, and a matching pulpit and reading desk.

One of the towers of Pennsylvania Castle rising from Church Knaps above the ruins of St Andrew's church, Portland. The Castle was built between 1797 and 1800 by John Penn, grandson of the founder of the American State that shares its name. The Castle, which is now a hotel, was later owned by John Sansom, who rose from being a quarryman to manager of Bath Stone Firms and one of the wealthiest men on Portland.

Portland Museum, Wakeham, from the entrance to Pennsylvania Castle. The Museum was opened in 1932 as a gift from Marie Stopes, the pioneer of birth control who had turned the old Higher Lighthouse into a summer home. The Museum is a delight, and was formed out of two cottages, one of which was built in 1640 and immortalised as Avice's Cottage by Thomas Hardy in *The Well Beloved*.

Portland Lighthouse and the sea mark on Portland Bill silhouetted at dusk. The waters off the Bill have always been regarded as amongst the most hazardous in the Channel. The shallow Shambles bank is nearby, and tide and current clash as they meet off the Bill, causing a race that can reach ten knots. Portland's first lighthouses were coal-fired and built in 1716, but the present 115 feet high (35 metres) lighthouse dates back to 1906. The derrick in the foreground is one of two used until recently to lower fishing boats into the waters off Broad Ope.

The old church at Fleet. On November 23rd 1824 the south-south-westerly wind battering the village on the edge of the East Fleet had reached storm force on a rising spring tide. The waves soon breached the Chesil, 'threatening terror to the most sheltered head, and awakening awe in the most callous heart.' The village was flooded, and all that now remains of the church is its chancel. The Great Gale marks the only occasion a ship was washed so high onto the Chesil that it was afterwards dragged over the summit of the beach and relaunched into Portland Roads.

Corton Farm and St Bartholomew's chapel, tucked under Corton Gap east of Portesham. The 13th century chapel contains its original stone altar, which is unusual as most were deliberately destroyed in the wake of the Reformation.

*Right* The upper Bride Valley, with bluebells flowering amidst the gorse.

*Below* The River Bride flowing past a cottage in Little Bredy.

*Below right* Bridehead House, Little Bredy, from above the cricket ground. The house was built by a London banker, Robert Williams, in the early 19th century, probably on the site of an earlier manor house belonging to Cerne Abbey. The house owes its name to the nearby springs that once marked the start of the River Bride, but which by damming now fill the lake beside the house.

Looking north from the most out-of-place monument in Dorset, that to Vice-Admiral Sir Thomas Masterman Hardy (1769-1839) at Black Down. The 72 feet high Portland stone tower, which resembles a factory chimney, commemorates Nelson's flag-captain on board HMS *Victory* at Trafalgar, and to whom the dying Admiral addressed his final words: 'Kiss me, Hardy'. Hardy was born at Kingston Russell, and spent his childhood in Portesham, from where he joined the Navy in 1781 as a thirteen-year-old captain's servant. He first came to Nelson's attention in 1796, when as a lieutenant aboard the *Minerve* he manned the ship's boat to rescue a sailor who had fallen overboard, and was himself then carried by the current towards the Spanish fleet. Nelson's words, which he spoke before going to Hardy's rescue, are almost the equal of those on his death-bed: 'By God, I'll not lose Hardy. Back the mizzen topsail!'

A brick and flint cottage close to the ford at Tarrant Monkton.

Cottages in West Street, Corfe Castle, with walls and roofs built from Purbeck limestone. Purbeck 'slates' are immensely heavy, weighing in at 1¼ tons per 100 square feet, which meant that they were often only used for a few courses above the eaves.

Dorset's farmhouses and cottages rank amongst its greatest glories. Because Dorset is largely agricultural, and the range of building materials is so great, they form an enduring architectural heritage few other counties can match.

The earliest surviving farmhouse is Barnston, near Corfe Castle, some of whose stone windows and walls date back to about 1280. The hall originally extended to the full height of the house, with an open hearth in its centre. One window retains its original stone seat and sills, as well as the hooks on which the shutters were hung before the introduction of glass. Barnston is almost a small manor house, and a much better example of how our medieval ancestors lived is to be found in the deserted village of Bardolfston, near Puddletown. Here the fallen grass-covered flint walls of 11 peasants' long-houses line what was the village street. The roofs would have been thatched. Some had two rooms, of which the larger was for livestock. Little yards at the back lead out into the ridge-and-furrow common fields that stretched up the sides of the valley.

From the late 16th century onwards an increasing number of houses of all styles and sizes survive. Outside Purbeck and Portland, where heavy stone slates provided the roofs, virtually all were originally thatched. Most cottages were only one room wide, whilst the longer farmhouses ran to three ground-floor rooms: a central hall with a fireplace, a parlour, and a kitchen and storeroom. Traditionally, both were built of local materials, including dressed stone, rubble stone, chalk, cob, flint, timber and brick. One of the joys of travelling round Dorset is to see how the materials change with the landscape, and the way in which the older houses sit so naturally in the countryside that surrounds them.

From the mid 18th century onwards two other styles of cottage began to be built. The first was the estate cottage, often still recognizable because those on each estate tend to be uniform, and because many bear their owner's coat-of-arms. The second was the deliberately picturesque, like the circular Umbrella Cottage at Lyme Regis and a handful of ornate lodges. The best known are the 24 identical cottages lining the main street in the model village of Milton Abbas, and which, despite their attractiveness, were built of cob – a mixture of mud and straw and the cheapest material available.

*Top* Umbrella Cottage, Lyme Regis, a seaside folly of about 1810.

*Above* Thatchers at work near Woodlands.

*Left* Abbey House, Tarrant Crawford. The brick wing was built in the 18th century, but the stone part may be a remnant of the once wealthy abbey founded by Richard Poore, Bishop of Salisbury, at the end of the 12th century.

One of the many lovely banded stone and flint cottages in Sydling St Nicholas.

Scoles Farm, near Kingston. The existing 17th century Purbeck rubble-stone farmhouse incorporates parts of a medieval hall-house. The 1244 Assize Rolls mention the payment of a pound of pepper by William de Scovill to the Constable of Corfe Castle in annual rent for his holding at the farm.

# THE PHOTOGRAPHS

Virtually all of the photographs in this book were taken specially for it over a two year period in an effort to try and evoke a portrait of Dorset as it is today. That meant exploring the county, by road, lane and footpath, in the hope of being able to find views and situations that would breathe fresh life into photographs of places that are already familiar and discover others that are little-known. There are few corners of the county that I haven't visited, and I am now certain of what I suspected at the outset, that Dorset is a treasure amongst counties. I hope these photographs will emphasise that point to those who have the power to manage and conserve its intrinsic beauty, as well as bringing joy to all who see them.

Taking the photographs has entailed a large amount of planning and travelling, many overnight stays, making appointments, and relying on fine weather: sometimes lucky, sometimes not. It has also given me immense pleasure in seeing, and learning about, Dorset and making many new friends in the process.

All of the photographs were taken on Kodachrome film, using a Nikon FE 35mm SLR camera, with a variety of lenses, ranging from a 20mm wide angle, to a 210mm telephoto. These lenses were mostly of fixed focal length, though a 70/210mm zoom was used for some of the telephoto shots. As for other equipment: I try not to use flash, unless it is essential, or helpful for filling in shadows; whereas a tripod is an invaluable asset, albeit a weight to carry around. One or two of the pictures have been 'enhanced' with a polarising filter, or a graduated blue; but given a free choice, I prefer to photograph when the light is right, and record what is actually there, rather than modifying it artificially.

I hope, in some of the pictures at least, that I have managed to include just those elements, both physical and emotional, which gave me a sense of purpose and pleasure at the moment of releasing the shutter, and that you will derive similar pleasure from looking at them.

JULIAN COMRIE

# ACKNOWLEDGEMENTS

A large number of people have helped in the creation of this book, and our thanks are due to them all. First and foremost, there are the people of Dorset who by chance appear in the photographs, either wittingly or unwittingly. Then there are those, listed below, who have generously helped by providing facilities for photography not normally available. Our principal regret is that lack of space has meant that we have only been able to include a fraction of the photographs.

Many published works have been drawn on for the text, but Jo Draper's *Dorset, the Complete Guide*, Arthur Oswald's *Country Houses of Dorset*, and the eight volumes of the Royal Commission on Historic Monument's survey of Dorset have been invaluable.

A particular debt is owed to booksellers throughout Dorset who have encouraged the project: without their support it would never have been started.

Amongst those who have helped us we must first mention Mr Christopher Chaplin for the miniature maps, Miss Louise Dobbs for the colour map, and Miss Elizabeth Dean for typing out the entire and often muddled text onto a word processor. But other debts are equally great, and we are grateful to Miss Helen Brotherton CBE; Graham and Lesley Burgess, of Wareham Forest Tourist Park; Mr Tom Coffin, of Holwell; Mr Patrick Darley and Miss Margaret Clapp, of Bridport-Gundry Plc; Jo Draper; Mrs R.H.Farquharson; Mr Barry Halton, of BP Exploration Operating Company Ltd; Mr Trevor Haysom, of W.J.Haysom, St Aldhelm's Quarry; Mr & Mrs Hudson, of Ashmore; Mr T.W.Jesty, of Silver Springs Watercress; Sir Mervyn Medlycott; Mrs J Moore, of Woodlands; Mr Stuart Morris; Mr Michael Oliver; Mr Roy Paul, of Giant's Head Caravan Park; Mr Trevor Poole and Mr Patrick Gould, of ARC Quarries Ltd; Mr Peter Pretlove, Heather Shearman, and the children of Sturminster Marshall First School, and Mr Robert Stephenson, Bandmaster; Dr Peyto Slatter; Mr Geoffrey Smith and Mr Peter Worrall, of Easton Masonry Co Ltd; Captain Nigel Thimbleby; Mrs Tupper, of Bagwell Farm Caravan Park; Mr Michael Venn, of The Ilchester Estates; Miss Lynda Williams, of Bournemouth International Airport; Mr John Young, of Humberts, Blandford Forum; and not forgetting the unidentified lady who gave Julian Comrie a lift to Maiden Newton when he foolishly grounded his car in a small invisible ditch.

Finally our deep and sincere thanks to Helen and Sarah, the two ladies who in our respective homes have supported and encouraged this book from conception, through gestation to its protracted birth. Without them it would simply not exist.

JULIAN COMRIE AND DAVID BURNETT

# INDEX

Looking west from Durdle Door to Bat's Head, with
Bull Rock offshore and Portland on the horizon.